ALTERNATIVE
MOVIE POSTERS
FILM ART FROM THE UNDERGROUND

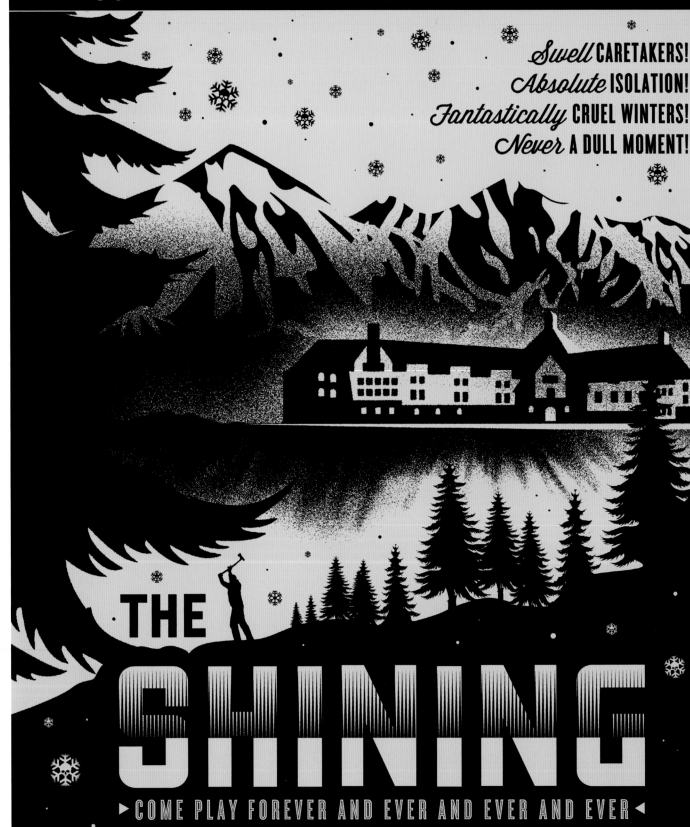

alternative
MOVIE POSTERS
matthew chojnacki

FILM ART
FROM THE
UNDERGROUND

Schiffer Publishing Ltd

4880 Lower Valley Road • Atglen, PA 19310

The Shining
18 x 24 in (46 x 61 cm)
Artist: Lure Design (page 18)

Film posters aren't *quite* what they used to be.

Only a few decades ago the motion picture industry was crafting an endless series of brilliant, head-turning film posters, drawing raves from both the art world and the public at large. Favorites included the classic, minimalist posters for *Rosemary's Baby* and *Vertigo*, the intricate comedic drawings of *Animal House* and *Life of Brian*, the brilliant comic book spoofs *Pulp Fiction* and *Mallrats*, and the chilling (at the time) one-sheets for *Jaws* and *The Exorcist*. Sometimes the quality of the posters even exceeded the films themselves: *Police Academy 4, 5, 6, 7*, anyone?

Regardless of the genre or quality of the film, each poster was given 110% by the graphic designers and photographers, painstakingly ensuring that their pieces properly conveyed the look and feel of the film. Movie posters single-handedly generated a real sense of excitement for a film's release. And if the film was worthy enough, you just *had* to own and hang your favorite one-sheet. My prized possession was a signed poster for *Sleepaway Camp* (!).

Then, in the mid-90s, priorities quickly shifted.

The film industry's intention for movie posters lost its way, seemingly becoming an afterthought. Instead of using paint brushes to create inventive works of art, they were instead using them to remove blemishes and wrinkles from celebrity headshots. The poster was reduced to simply communicating *who* was in the film, instead of conveying the bigger picture—the spirit of the film. This could have been due to cost-cutting, disinterest, or lack of original material (see Hollywood's endless stream of '80s remakes). But whatever the rationale, the results were bad. Really bad.

This was unfortunate for hardcore filmgoers. You know, the ones geeking out at film fests and collectors shows, and salivating at those countless hours of special features on Blu-ray and DVD. Count me in this group. But as film studios directed their attention away from movie posters, these same film buffs took matters into their own hands. They started to pick up their pens, pencils, and paintbrushes, crafting their own pieces for their favorite flicks. The alternative movie poster "crusade" had begun.

What started out as mere fan art has now turned into a thriving and influential platform, with art houses such as Mondo leading the way with a steady stream of stunning releases. Art galleries also began to take note, bringing this new medium to the forefront (see Gallery 1988 in Los Angeles, Spoke Art in San Francisco, and Bottleneck Gallery in NYC, for example).

The art underground has crawled into the mainstream, generating hundreds of posters each year, selling initially for $20 of $30 in very limited quantities, which in turn have generated hundreds, sometimes thousands of dollars per piece among collectors. Underground film posters are now in much more demand than anything official emanating from the studios themselves.

And rightly so. This new wave of designers is once again crafting stunning pieces not witnessed since the '70s and '80s. This talented group of artists has brought back the techniques of long-revered poster icons such as Drew Struzan (*Star Wars, Back to the Future, Raiders of the Lost Ark*) and Saul Bass (*Anatomy of a Murder, The Man with the Golden Arm*), along with their own new and inventive approaches.

Poster art is clearly back with a vengeance.

I spent a year combing through more than ten thousand images, and upwards of a thousand designers, to curate this collection of 100+ alternative film poster designers and their finest pieces.

Some were commissioned by film fests and theaters, others were created for art galleries or periodicals, and still more were designed specifically for this book. All are masterpieces from across the globe, created by amazing and eclectic artists that share a common bond—mixing design and film in a blender, with stunning results.

You will also see that each artist is profiled alongside their pieces. Feel free to reach out to them! Many are available for commissions and also welcome random e-mails of appreciation or inquiry.

I hope that you enjoy looking back on some of your favorite films through an entirely new lens.

–Matthew Chojnacki

BEHIND THE POSTERS: The influence for *Ms. 45* was exploitation films, but also trying to imagine the shock value if this poster had been released in 1981. We have become very desensitized to sex and violence since then. When I was growing up in the '80s, movies like *Ms. 45* were supposed to be off limits to kids...but of course I watched them all. My very first job was at a video store when I was 15. My mom knew the owner and they paid me under the table (I rewound videos and returned them to the shelves). I had access to so many films that I probably shouldn't have seen.

I'm a big fan of *Leon* [right]. Working on a poster for a film that you appreciate is always rewarding. This was also one of Gary Oldman's best performances—a very memorable villain:

"Benny, bring me everyone."

"What do you mean, everyone?"

"EVERYONE!!!"

The influence for the *Leon* poster was the relationship between Leon and Matilda. Leon was the forced protector of innocence, but was a child himself in many ways. It's a great movie, but as you watch it, there's a little voice in the back of your head that's going, "this relationship is a little creepy."

More artwork from James Rheem Davis on pages 92 and 93.

Laurie Shipley

Revenge of the Cheerleaders
11 x 17 in (28 x 43 cm)

LOCATION Durham, North Carolina / US

SITE Laurieshipley.com

BEHIND THE POSTER: I was invited to design a poster for *Revenge of the Cheerleaders* by Matt Pennachi, who was running Cinema Overdrive at the time. Every month these guys played an old B movie on 35mm film at the Colony Theatre in Raleigh, North Carolina, and had a different local artist design a screen printed poster to go along with the event. I am also a fan of the film! It's hilarious and the poster was well received.

INFLUENCES: Cinematically speaking, some of my favorite directors are Tim Burton, David Lynch, and Jim Henson.
FAVORITE FILM / GENRE: You can take a pretty good guess at the stuff I gravitate toward from my answer above, but, if I had to say just one, I'd definitely have to pick David Lynch's *Blue Velvet*.
PREFERRED MEDIUM: Pencils, computer, and fabric.

Street Trash
24 x 36 in (61 x 91 cm)
A Mondo release

LOCATION Toronto, Ontario / Canada

SITE Ghoulishgary.com

INFLUENCES: I'm heavily influenced by horror films. Working at a horror magazine for 13+ years will do that to you. But I was a dyed in the wool horror fan before the magazine was even a glint in my eye.

My list of influences is long and varied, but certainly Basil Gogos, Matthew Peak, Robert Gleason, Reynold Brown, Saul Bass, and Bernie Wrightston grabbed me when I was a kid. Modern artists like Charles Burns, Ken Taylor, Martin Ansin, Tom "The Dudedesigns" Hodge, Phantom City Creative, and Jason Edmiston are all also creating incredibly inspired work.

FAVORITE FILM / GENRE: Horror, gangster, and comedies, mostly from the '70s and '80s.
FIRST FILM: It was probably *Godzilla* or a Universal Monsters film. There was a cable access show out of Cleveland that used to air all of the classic monster movies.
PREFERRED MEDIUM: Screen printing, but I will always love my trusty pencils, pens, and ink.
ADDITIONAL REMARKS: I feel very fortunate to make a living drawing images that I love. Long live poster illustration!

More artwork from Ghoulish Gary Pullin on pages 40 and 41.

MEL GIBSON
JOANNE SAMUEL
AND
HUGH KEAYES-BYRNE
IN A FILM BY
GEORGE MILLER

BEHIND THE POSTER: Trevor at The Silver Screen Society asked me to contribute a piece for them. I hadn't seen *Mad Max* before that either, which was one of the cool aspects about working on the poster. Since I hadn't seen it first, I didn't have the affection or premeditation that others may have approached it with.

INFLUENCES: Right now, Charlie Brown. But also my Wacom tablet, Pee-Wee Herman, tacos, David Byrne, coffee, John Heartfield, Paul Thomas Anderson, family, the color black, Dustin Hoffman, friends, comedy, Bob Gill, The Coen Brothers, pubs, Bill Withers, New York, beer, Muppets, James Victore, Marlon Brando, Al Pacino, laughing, Carol Kane, Jay Shaw, Ferris Bueller, Parra, Spike Lee, street

art, art history, screen printing, Bill Cosby, Stanley Kubrick, The Pope of Greenwich Village, hockey, the Pixies, Kermit the Frog, Buffalo, Ray and Charles Eames, Milton Glaser, Hillman Curtis. At least a hundred other things, too.

FAVORITE FILM / GENRE: I have three favorite movies. *True Romance*, *Dog Day Afternoon*, and *Jules and Jim*.

ADDITIONAL REMARKS: I was surprised to learn how different the alternative poster scene is from doing studio theatrical posters (which I also design). I enjoy the challenge. It's having a wonderful effect on movie poster art overall.

More artwork from Derek Gabryszak on page 173

Invasion of the Body Snatchers
18 × 24 in (46 × 61 cm)

LOCATION Broomfield, Colorado / US
SITE Kingdomofnonsense.com

A Robert H. Solo Production of A Philip Kaufman Film
Donald Sutherland · Brooke Adams · Leonard Nimoy
Jeff Goldblum · Veronica Cartwright
Screenplay by W.D. Richter, Based on the novel "The Body Snatchers" by Jack Finney
Produced by Robert H. Solo   Directed by Philip Kaufman

of the Body Snatchers

INFLUENCES: I find myself constantly influenced and inspired by fellow poster artists. There are so many talented people out there. Webuyyourkids, Tomer Hanuka, Rob Jones, Jason Munn, Aesthetic Apparatus, Rich Kelly, Martin Ansin, and Kilian Eng are some of my heroes.

I'm also heavily influenced by past artists like Wiktor Gorka, Eryk Lipinski, Marek Mosinski, Jan Lenica, and Jerzy Flisak. All brilliant.

FAVORITE FILM / GENRE: *Romancing the Stone*, horror.
FIRST FILM: The first film I remember watching was *Magic* with Anthony Hopkins. Did a real number on me. Haven't seen it again since.
PREFERRED MEDIUM: I work mostly in digital, but my favorite medium is pen and ink.
ADDITIONAL REMARKS: "One day, someone showed me a glass of water that was half full. And he said, 'Is it half full or half empty?' So I drank the water. No more problem." –Alejandro Jodorowsky

More artwork from Jay Shaw on page 33

Viktor Hertz

Coffee and Cigarettes
28 × 39 in (70 × 100 cm)

LOCATION	Uppsala / Sweden
SITE	Viktorhertz.com

Coffee and cigarettes
A film by Jim Jarmusch

Starring Roberto Benigni, Steven Wright, Joie Lee, Cinqué Lee, Steve Buscemi, Iggy Pop, Tom Waits, Joe Rigano, Vinny Vella, Vinny Vella JR., Renée French, E.J. Rodriguez, Alex Descas, Isaach de Bankolé, Cate Blanchett, Meg White, Jack White, Alfred Molina, Steve Coogan, GZA, RZA, Bill Murray, Bill Rice, Taylor Mead

BEHIND THE POSTER: I was playing around with ideas [for *Coffee and Cigarettes*] until I realized that I could include a coffee mug and a cigarette in an ampersand, which was somewhat of an "aha experience." It's one of my favorite posters, and was the first to travel around the Internet for a bit.

INFLUENCES: Stanley Kubrick, Woody Allen, Noma Bar, Autechre, Salvador Dalí, Alfred Hitchcock, Charlie Chaplin, Olly Moss, Aphex Twin. I am influenced by different forms of expression, like music, film, and advertising, but also random shapes and figures.

FAVORITE FILM / GENRE: Good science fiction.

FIRST FILM: I remember my mom letting me watch *Goodfellas* when I was home from school sick one day. I was about eleven. *A Clockwork Orange* was also an early encounter with film as an art form.

PREFERRED MEDIUM: I work entirely in Illustrator, with vector-based graphics. I'm also interested in expanding to other mediums, like motion graphics and film.

ADDITIONAL REMARKS: Thanks for reading! Feel free to contact me if you'd like to collaborate on a project.

More artwork from Viktor Hertz on pages 88, 89, and 134

12

Heathers
Unprinted / personal work

Chris Thornley

ALIAS Raid71
LOCATION Darwen / UK
SITE Raid71.com

BEHIND THE POSTER: *Heathers* was me just mucking around with an idea. I've always enjoyed the film, so this design was just a bit of fun.

INFLUENCES: I have a long list of influences and pick things up from everywhere. However, if I had to choose people: David Hockney for the way he plays with conventions and Terry Gilliam for his sense of humor.

FAVORITE FILM / GENRE: Science fiction or fantasy.

FIRST FILM: I'd like to say it was something cool, but it was probably one of the *Herbie* films. I do also remember seeing *Bambi* and getting very upset.

PREFERRED MEDIUM: My job dictates digital, as it's easier for projects.

ADDITIONAL REMARKS: I love working on film posters. There are so many elements to play around with and to consider. Plus I'm lucky enough to watch films while I work!

More artwork from Chris Thornley on pages 72 and 150

Jesse Philips

LOCATION Albuquerque, New Mexico / US

SITE jessephilips.com

Iron Man
24 x 36 in (61 x 91 cm)
A Mondo release

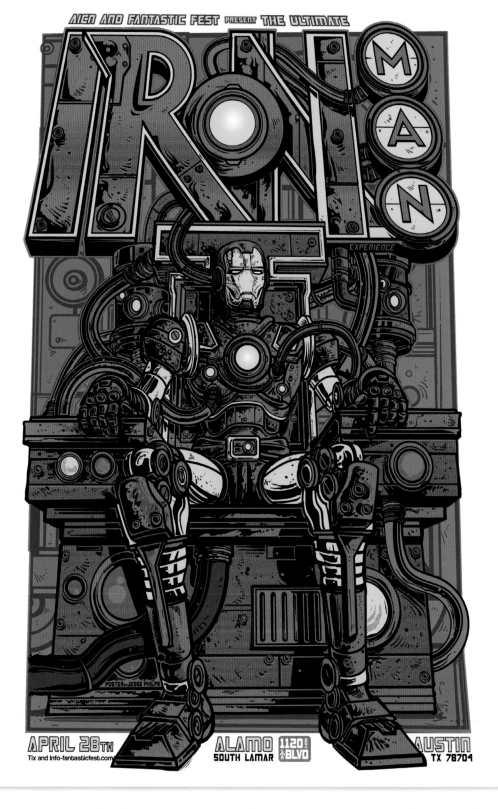

BEHIND THE POSTERS: I was first contacted by Tim Doyle and Rob Jones [of Mondo] back in 2006 to work on an event poster for Alamo Drafthouse's Fantastic Fest. They had discovered my concert posters on GigPosters.com and liked my giant robot-themed imagery. That was followed up by *The Transformers* movie poster in 2007, and *Iron Man* (seen here) in 2008.

For *Tommy* [right], Rob Jones came to me with a specific idea of portraying the Acid Queen/Iron Maiden character from the movie. I then decided to incorporate pinball play-field elements into the design. Generally the design process is pretty open-ended

with Mondo. I first submit sketches and ideas. From there the idea is chosen and refined until everyone is satisfied with the concept. I then finalize the design.

INFLUENCES: Some of my earliest influences were reading Marvel and DC comics in the early '80s, as well as *Mad* magazine; *Mad*'s Jack Davis was particularly influential. And, of course, there were the '80s cartoons (*G.I. Joe*, *Transformers*, *He-Man*, etc.). Also, on a trip to Japan, when I was eight years old, I discovered manga (Japanese comics), which cemented a lifelong obsession with Japanese culture, art, and design.

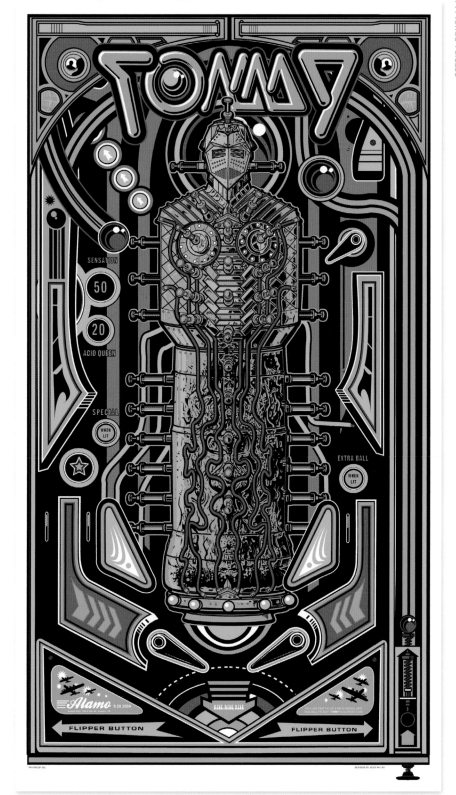

Tommy
20 × 36 in (51 × 91 cm)
A Mondo release

▶ Jesse Philips

LOCATION Albuquerque, New Mexico / US
SITE Jessephilips.com

Artist influences: Katsuhiro Otomo, Katsuya Terada, Yoshitaka Amano, Jean Giraud Moebius, Hirohiko Araki, and many more.

Directors: Stanley Kubrick, Ridley Scott, Guillermo del Toro, The Coen Brothers, Robert Rodriguez, Quentin Tarantino.

FAVORITE FILM / GENRE: As you can see by the directors I've listed, I like visually rich films. Sci-fi, fantasy, drama, violence, etc.

FIRST FILM: My mom took me to see *Return of the Jedi* in '83. I also have many fond memories seeing movies at the drive-in theater in my parents' pop-top VW Bus, many times instead peering at the R-rated movies that were playing on adjacent screens.

PREFERRED MEDIUM: Pen and ink, vector graphics.

ADDITIONAL REMARKS: Thanks to everyone that's given me the opportunity to create movie posters over the years. I hope to create many more in the future.

Eternal Sunshine of the Spotless Mind
17 x 23 in (42 x 59 cm - A2)

LOCATION Belfast, Ireland

SITE Peterstrain.co.uk (represented by Début Art UK & US - Debutart.com)

BEHIND THE POSTERS: After college, I wanted to forge a career in illustration, but also needed to develop my style of working. So, I started making film posters and these were two of the first. I'm a huge fan of both films, so it made sense to focus on something that I was passionate about to aid in the experimentation.

INFLUENCES: Directors: Wes Anderson, Stanley Kubrick, Michel Gondry, Edgar Wright, Quentin Tarantino, and Christopher Nolan. Artists: Paul Davis, David Shrigley, Joe Wilson, Steven Forbes, and various street artists. Actors: Bill Murray, Jack Nicholson, Leonardo DiCaprio, and Cillian Murphy.

Peter Strain

LOCATION Belfast, Ireland

SITE Peterstrain.co.uk (represented by Début Art UK & US — Debutart.com)

FAVORITE FILM / GENRE: I don't think that I have a definite favorite film, but *Eternal Sunshine of the Spotless Mind, Being John Malkovich, The Shining, Rushmore,* and *The Life Aquatic with Steve Zissou* would all be up there. These will probably change again next week.

FIRST FILM: *Beauty and the Beast.*
PREFERRED MEDIUM: I tend to use pen, ink, and pencil first. I then scan all of the elements to clean them up and color them digitally.

POSTER: LUREDESIGINC.COM

Lure Design

Pink Flamingos
24 x 36 in (61 x 91 cm)
Die-cut

DESIGNERS Sarah Blacksher and Jeff Matz

LOCATION Orlando, Florida / US

SITE Luredesigninc.com

BEHIND THE POSTERS: [Sarah]: *The Shining* [see page 2] scared the hair off of my head when I was a kid. As an adult I found it to be a bit humorous and wanted to portray that by making the poster a fun "travel" advertisement.

[Jeff]: *Pink Flamingos* [shown here] is a true cult classic, and I thought that it would be an interesting challenge to try to make the poster as offensive as the movie.

INFLUENCES: Blurting them out at random: Stanley Kubrick, Saul Bass, Frank Lloyd Wright, Wes Anderson, Robert Rauschenberg, Charles & Ray Eames, Andy Warhol, Alfred Hitchcock, Art Chantry, Charles Anderson, and Woody Pirtle.

FIRST FILM: [Sarah]: The first film that made me take notice was *Creepshow*. Its execution (and the way it was broken down into shorts) really impressed me...not to mention that I loved Ted Danson from *Cheers*.

[Jeff]: The first film-going experience that really impacted me was *Tora! Tora! Tora!*, with my father and brother—a big night out for a seven-year-old. It was the first time that I was engrossed in a film's story and brought into the action due to the scale of the big screen.

PREFERRED MEDIUM: Ink-slingin' for life! We're lucky to love what we do and lucky to have access to a screen printing table all day, every day.

18

Eraserhead
16 × 24 in (41 × 61 cm)

A DAVID LYNCH FILM

ERASER HEAD

JACK NANCE
CHARLOTTE STEWART
ALLEN JOSEPH

LOCATION Rochester, New York / US
SITE Adammaida.com

BEHIND THE POSTER: I was painting one day, messing about with some thumbprints from ink. I noticed one in particular that took shape of what appeared to me as Henry Spencer's hair. It didn't necessarily have anything particular to do with the film. But in their own ways, most of David Lynch's films seem to always find their own path back to us. I thought that the thumbprint in itself was relevant enough in that aspect to warrant the use of it in the piece. I then just built the imagery around that.

INFLUENCES: Too many to name really. So I'll think of the first four that come to mind: Roman Cieślewicz, Andrzej Pagowski, Stanley Kubrick, and Shigeo Fukuda.
FAVORITE FILM / GENRE: Any that leaves me longing to watch it just one more time.
PREFERRED MEDIUM: Silkscreen. Something about being in control of how a piece is made, from inception to production.

Step Brothers
(actual title = John Stamos)
18 × 24 in (46 × 61 cm)

BEHIND THE POSTERS: *John Stamos* was for a *Step Brothers* tribute show at Gallery 1988 in L.A. *Beetlejuice, Beetlejuice, Beetlejuice!* [right] was part of Three Barrels, Ltd.'s "Trick-or-Treat for UNICEF" Halloween series, with proceeds from sales going to UNICEF. Both posters are sold out.

INFLUENCES: I get a lot of my inspiration from comic book illustrators such as Art Adams, Ryan Ottley, Steve McNiven, and Joe Madureira, but that list can go on forever. My favorite contemporary poster designer is COOP, and my personal hero would probably be Stan Winston for his ability to create such iconic silhouettes. I also find the multifacetedness and design philosophies of Isamu Noguchi and Charles and Ray Eames very influential.

Beetlejuice
(actual title = Beetlejuice, Beetlejuice, Beetlejuice!)
24 x 36 in (61 x 91 cm)
Glow-in-the-dark ink

FAVORITE FILM / GENRE: Basically any zombie movie or any action-adventure from the '80s. All-time favorite would probably be *Predator* (1987).

FIRST FILM: *The Monster Squad* (1987)

PREFERRED MEDIUM: Mac, Adobe Illustrator, Adobe Photoshop, Cintiq.

ADDITIONAL REMARKS: I try my best to stay as true to the content as possible through concept and execution and hopefully art and film fans appreciate this.

Saw
15 × 20 in (38 × 51 cm)

LOCATION Portland, Oregon / US

SITE Nickstokesdesign.com

cut here

SAW

BEHIND THE POSTER: The first *Saw* is great. I love the simplicity, concept, and execution of the film. It is also filled with a lot of great iconography. I thought it would be a fun challenge to try and reduce the story and icons into a single image that would communicate the film's general plot.

INFLUENCES: Some of my biggest contemporary influences are Jeremyville, The Little Friends of Printmaking, Always with Honor, and Mike Perry. I also love a lot of the mid-century guys like M. Sasek, Paul Rand, and Saul Bass. I am drawn to bold and colorful imagemaking.

FAVORITE FILM / GENRE: I love '80s action movies. Anything starring Arnold, Bruce, or Mel is most likely sitting on my shelf. I am also a big fan of darker concept-driven movies like *Alien*, *Moon*, *12 Monkeys,* and *Looper.*

FIRST FILM: Probably *Wayne's World,* or the first *Ninja Turtles.* I still own both on VHS and watch them yearly.

PREFERRED MEDIUM: Digital, although I am starting to do a lot more work traditionally.

ADDITIONAL REMARKS: I'm stoked to be in the same book as The Little Friends of Printmaking!

White Men Can't Jump
27 × 40 in (69 × 102 cm)

Michael Weinstein

LOCATION Cambridge, Massachusetts / US

SITE Michael-weinstein.com

BEHIND THE POSTER: I noticed a lot of people doing redesigns for superhero films and big action movies. I was looking for something a little more obscure that hadn't been done before, and I love basketball, so the movie stuck with me. I remember thinking the Reebok Pump sneakers that Billy Hoyle (Woody Harrelson) wears in the movie were awesome, and thought that Wesley Snipes' character pumping them up for him was a good metaphor for the film.

INFLUENCES: Olly Moss had a great set of movie poster designs with a black, white, and red color scheme that inspired me to try a minimalist approach for the poster. The lettering style for the film title was inspired by Saul Bass' poster for *The Man with the Golden Arm*.
FAVORITE FILM / GENRE: I love comedies, but my favorite movie is *City of God*.
FIRST FILM: I vaguely remember *The Goonies, Honey, I Shrunk the Kids,* and *The Land Before Time* getting a lot of play in my house.
PREFERRED MEDIUM: Vector graphics.
ADDITIONAL REMARKS: You can put a cat in an oven, but that don't make it a biscuit.

Big
17 × 23 in (42 × 59 cm - A2)

LOCATION London, UK
SITE Danielnorris.tumblr.com

ZOLTAR SPEAKS

A PENNY MARSHALL FILM

BiG

TOM HANKS, ELIZABETH PERKINS
AND ROBERT LOGGIA

DAN NORRIS

BEHIND THE POSTERS: I am a kid of the '80s, so these films mean a lot to me and seemed like a natural fit.

INFLUENCES: Alan Fletcher, Saul Bass, Stephen Gammell, John Heartfield, Abram Games, Noma Bar, Frank Miller, Tang Yau Hoong…for different reasons they all inspire me. I also love what Olly Moss has been up to recently.

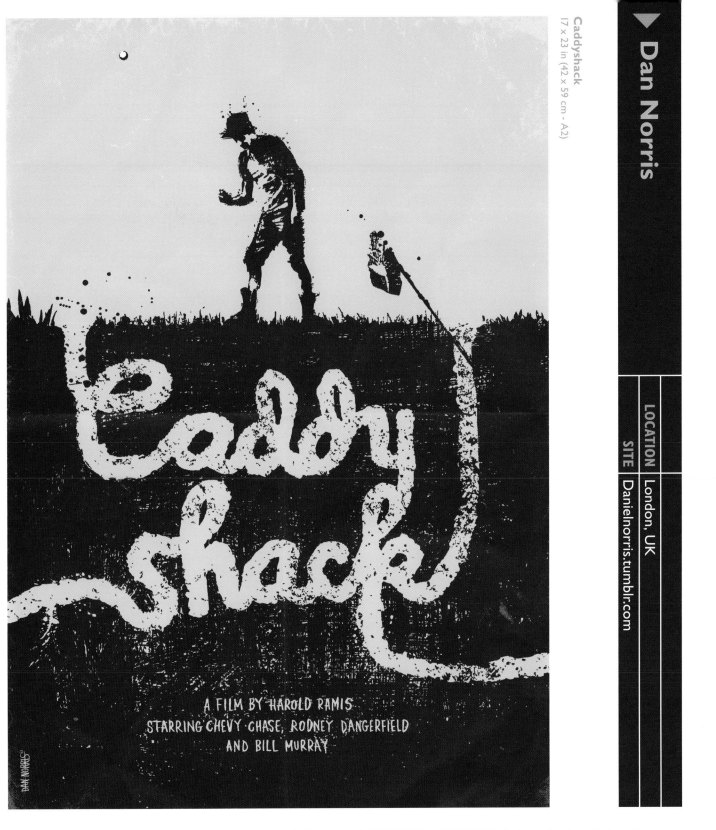

FAVORITE FILM / GENRE: *The Goonies*. Such a special film.
FIRST FILM: *The Flame and the Arrow*, the '50s, Burt Lancaster classic.

PREFERRED MEDIUM: Paint/ink, then digital allows me complete creative freedom.
ADDITIONAL REMARKS: I aim to use wit and imagination to create designs that live long in the memory.

Psycho
18 × 24 in (46 × 61 cm)

DESIGNERS Dave Windisch and Stacy Curtis
LOCATION Chicago, Illinois, and Indianapolis, Indiana / US
SITE Mile44.com

BEHIND THE POSTERS: *Holy Grail* [right] is almost like a friendship test movie. "Oh, you can quote *Holy Grail*? Then, yes, let's hang out." It's like a secret handshake.

INFLUENCES: [Dave]: So many artists to reference: Saul Bass, classic jazz record covers, war bond posters, Polish poster art, Bill Watterson, Tyler Stout, Olly Moss, Studio Ghibli, and a lot of time spent digging through record crates at Luna Records in Indianapolis.

FAVORITE FILM / GENRE: [Dave]: *The African Queen, Jaws, The Thin Man, The Godfather,* and *The Empire Strikes Back* always reside in my top movie list of all time. I love classic horror flicks—the Universal Monsters. Also, sci-fi B movies, late night horror host films of Svengooli and Sammy Terry, '70s drive-in films...it's all over the place.

Monty Python and the Holy Grail
18 x 24 in (46 x 61 cm)

DESIGNERS	Dave Windisch and Stacy Curtis
LOCATION	Chicago, Illinois, and Indianapolis, Indiana / US
SITE	Mile44.com

FIRST FILM: [Dave]: *Raiders of the Lost Ark*. I went with my mom, dad, and sister and remember not being able to completely watch the face melting scene. I was seven and remember coming home and being too scared to enter my dark room. Dad had to turn the light on for me.

PREFERRED MEDIUM: Our screen-printed posters are designed with a mix of pen and ink, Rubylith, and Photoshop, all mixed up and used as needed.

ADDITIONAL REMARKS: [Dave]: It's nice to see alternative film posters dominating the movie poster world. I collect original theatrical posters and the art of interpreting an entire movie in one sheet of paper is nearly lost today.

More artwork from Mile 44 on page 104

Jason Edmiston

▶ A **Nightmare on Elm Street 3: Dream Warriors**
18 x 24 in (46 x 61 cm)
A Mondo release

LOCATION Toronto, Ontario / Canada

SITE jasonedmiston.com

BEHIND THE POSTERS: I'm drawn to horror movies and their characters. I love drawing all those nooks and crannies! These two movies have great villains, terrific costumes, and inventive action scenes that leave a lasting impression.

INFLUENCES: Artists: Frank Frazetta, Basil Gogos, Norman Rockwell, The Hildebrandt Brothers, Boris Vallejo, James Bama, Ron English, Shawn Barber, Anita Kunz, Roberta Parada, Ken Taylor, Justin Erickson, Gary Pullin...the list goes on.

Directors: Wes Craven, Steven Spielberg, Quentin Tarantino, John Carpenter, Dario Argento, Martin Scorsese, Ridley Scott, The Coen Brothers.

Art Directors: Any art director that allows the artist to "do their thing," with just enough pushing to keep their game up. My favorite art director ever is Rob Jones of Mondo (a great artist in his own right).

▶ Jason Edmiston

Maniac Cop 2
18 x 24 in (46 x 61 cm)
A Mondo release

LOCATION | Toronto, Ontario / Canada
SITE | Jasonedmiston.com

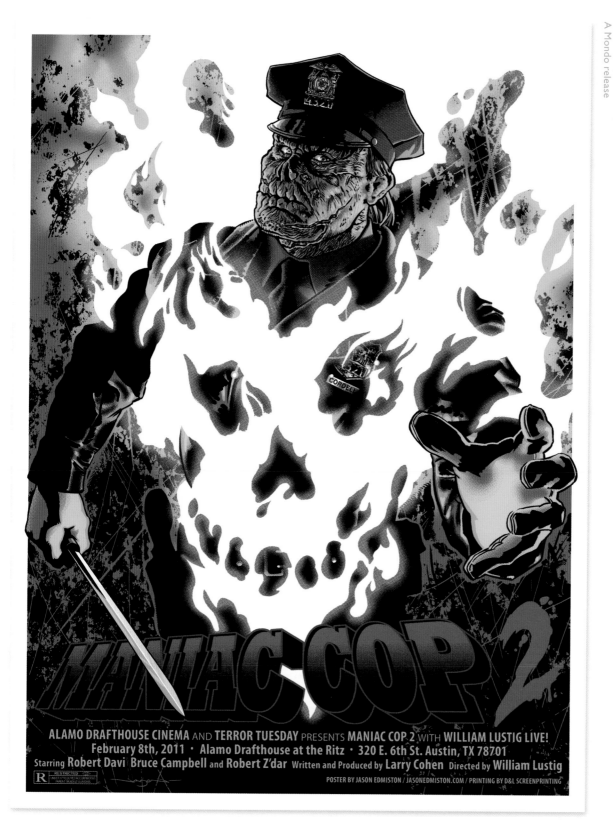

FAVORITE FILM / GENRE: Horror. *A Nightmare on Elm Street* or *The Exorcist*, but I also have a sweet spot for anything James Bond.
FIRST FILM: That made an impact? *Star Wars*.
PREFERRED MEDIUM: Acrylic.

ADDITIONAL REMARKS: I love the art of illustrated movie posters, and am glad to see the return to handmade designs. I have grown very tired of the "floating heads" created in Photoshop that have been the norm for the last 20 years.

Jason Munn

Bonnie and Clyde
18 x 24 in (46 × 61 cm)
A Mondo release

LOCATION Oakland, California / US

SITE jasonmunn.com

BONNIE and CLYDE

JUNE 18, 2011 ALAMO DRAFTHOUSE CINEMA PRESENTS THE TEXAS MONTHLY ROLLING ROADSHOW PILOT POINT, TX

BEHIND THE POSTERS: Both of these posters were part of the Alamo Drafthouse's Texas Monthly Rolling Roadshow 2011 series. There were ten films total, all of which had a connection to the state of Texas.

INFLUENCES: Mid-century design and designers.
PREFERRED MEDIUM: Screen print.

TENDER
MERCIES

JUNE 19, 2011 **ALAMO DRAFTHOUSE CINEMA PRESENTS THE TEXAS MONTHLY ROLLING ROADSHOW** WAXAHACHIE, TX

▶ Jason Munn

Tender Mercies
18 x 24 in (46 x 61 cm)
A Mondo release

LOCATION Oakland, California / US
SITE Jasonmunn.com

Being John Malkovich
17 x 23 in (42 x 59 cm - A2)

LOCATION Melbourne, Victoria / Australia

SITE Heathkillen.com

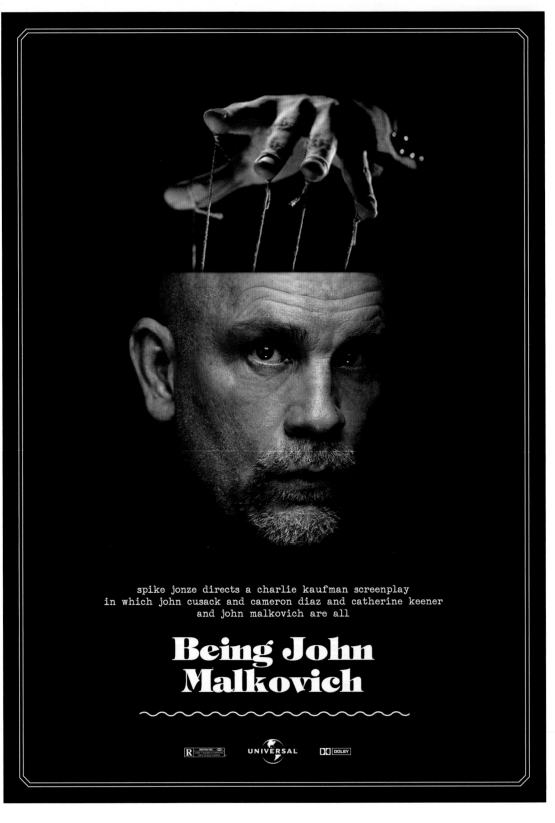

INFLUENCES: I have a broad range of influences and my tastes are quite diverse. I'm drawn to strong, iconic imagery as well as worlds that are exquisitely crafted. I'm also strongly drawn to naturalistic films. A recent film that beautifully captures all of these elements is *Never Let Me Go*.

FIRST FILM: My parents took me to films while I was still a baby (including *The Amityville Horror*, I'm told), but the first film that I can recall seeing was *Return of the Jedi*, back when screenings still had intermissions. I can still remember that experience fairly clearly. **PREFERRED MEDIUM:** Everything ends up on the computer, but I always sketch ideas first, and I like to work with mixed media. Whatever's right for the project.

More artwork from Heath Killen on pages 66 and 67

▶ Jay Shaw

Rocky III
24 × 18 in (61 × 46 cm)
A Mondo release

LOCATION Broomfield, Colorado / US

SITE Kingdomofnonsense.com

Continued from page 11

BEHIND THE POSTER: Mondo asked me if I'd like to create a *Rocky III* poster for Alamo Drafthouse's "Summer of '82" series. I agreed without a second thought.

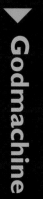

Tales from the Crypt
18 x 24 in (46 x 61 cm)

LOCATION Wales / UK

SITE Godmachine.co.uk

BEHIND THE POSTERS: I was approached by clients and galleries to create these posters and was luckily a fan of both films.

INFLUENCES: Lynch, Morphine, Beardsley, Chris Isaak, Tom Waits, 80% of everything I see and hear.

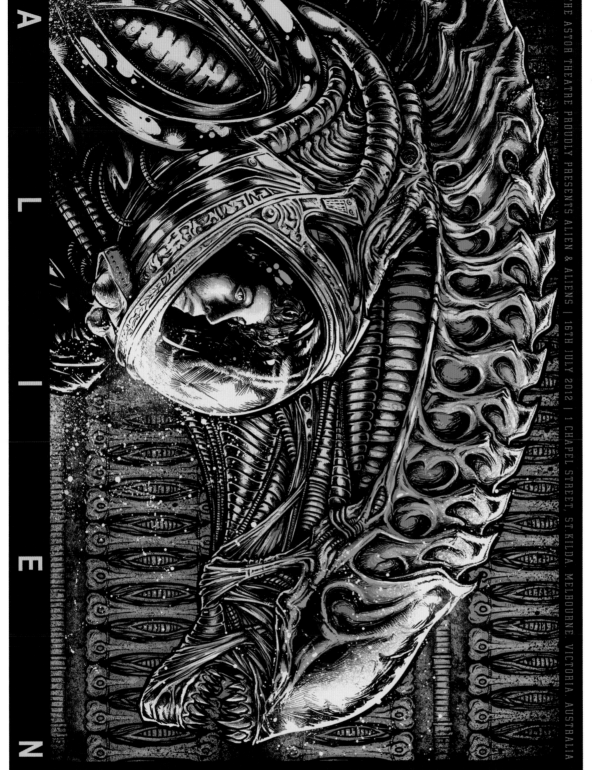

Alien
24 × 18 in (61 × 46 cm)

THE ASTOR THEATRE PROUDLY PRESENTS ALIEN & ALIENS | 16TH JULY 2012 | 1 CHAPEL STREET, ST KILDA, MELBOURNE, VICTORIA, AUSTRALIA

LOCATION	Wales / UK
SITE	Godmachine.co.uk

FAVORITE FILM / GENRE: *Repo Man, Master and Commander, Event Horizon*...it's eclectic at best.

PREFERRED MEDIUM: Computer or pen and paper.
ADDITIONAL REMARKS: If you want to be better than anyone else, be kinder than anyone else.

Todd Slater

Close Encounters of the Third Kind
24 x 36 in (61 x 91 cm)
A Mondo release

LOCATION	Austin, Texas / US
SITE	Toddslater.net

BEHIND THE POSTER: It was commissioned by Mondotees. They knew that I like science fiction and thought it would be a good fit for me. The first time I saw the film was in an arcade, which probably had something to do with the art.

INFLUENCES: For painting I like Jenny Saville and Steven Assael along with many other figurative painters. My favorite directors include Wes Anderson, Paul Thomas Anderson, and David Fincher. Without a doubt, my favorite art director is Rob Jones, who designs everything you see for Jack White. He never hesitates to tell me when something I've made is awful and every artist needs that.

FAVORITE FILM / GENRE: Science fiction, of course.
FIRST FILM: It was *E.T.* at a drive-in theater, I'm told.
PREFERRED MEDIUM: Silkscreen printing.

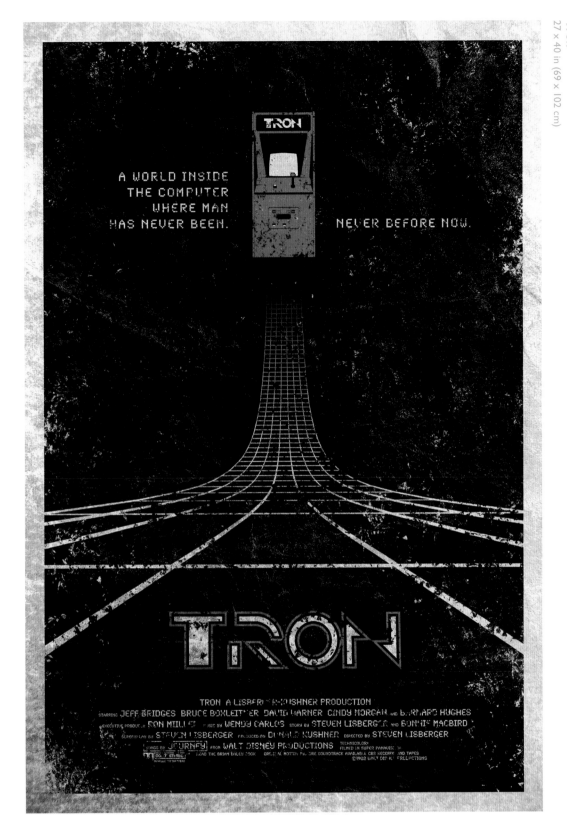

BEHIND THE POSTER: *Tron*, to me, has always been a world that I would love to visit. There's something about the dark atmosphere and glowing lights that calms me.

INFLUENCES: I love the work of Olly Moss, Tom Whalen, Ken Taylor, and Martin Ansin, to name a few. Some of my favorite directors are Steven Spielberg, David Fincher, Fritz Lang, and Christopher Nolan. I'm always impressed by any filmmaker who can make me forget that I'm watching a film.

FAVORITE FILM / GENRE: My favorite films are *The Shawshank Redemption* and *The Thing*, and my favorite genres are horror and science fiction.

FIRST FILM: *An American Tale*. I was 2 years old. I only remember bits and pieces, except of course for that terrifying mouse machine.

PREFERRED MEDIUM: Digital.

ADDITIONAL REMARKS: "Creativity is allowing yourself to make mistakes. Art is knowing which ones to keep." –Scott Adams

More artwork from Adam Rabalais on pages 152 and 153

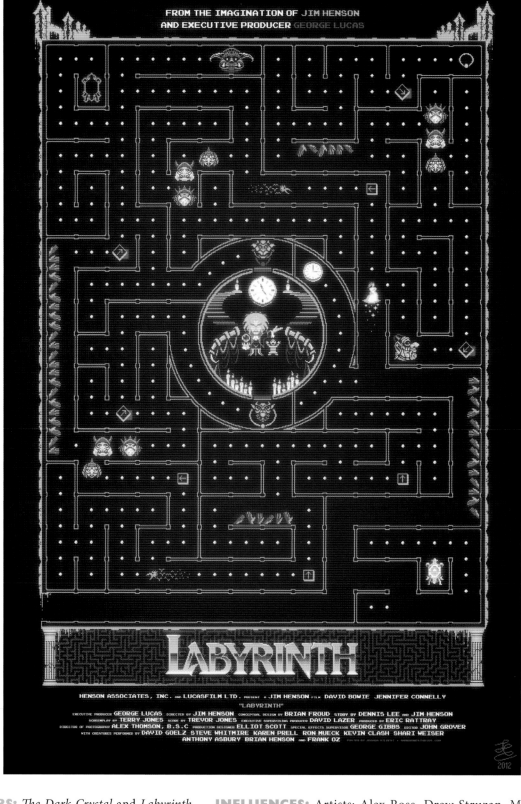

BEHIND THE POSTERS: *The Dark Crystal* and *Labyrinth* [right] were both a big part of my childhood. I began these shortly after my first successful TeeFury submission [TeeFury is an indie tee shirt retailer producing a unique design daily]. Mashing up *Pac-Man* with *Labyrinth* was the starting point, and in the midst of working on it the idea of doing the same with *Donkey Kong* and *The Dark Crystal* came to me. The resulting *Skeksi Kong* was then accepted by TeeFury as well.

INFLUENCES: Artists: Alex Ross, Drew Struzan, Michael Turner, Jack Kirby, Bruce Timm, Darwyn Cooke, Frank Miller. Directors: Steven Spielberg, James Cameron, Christopher Nolan, Guillermo del Toro, Peter Jackson, Sergio Leone, Hayao Miyazaki. **FAVORITE FILM / GENRE:** Action/adventure and sci-fi/ fantasy.

The Dark Crystal
(actual title = Skeksi Kong)
13 x 19 in (33 x 48 cm)

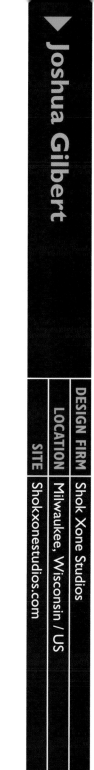

Joshua Gilbert

DESIGN FIRM	Shok Xone Studios
LOCATION	Milwaukee, Wisconsin / US
SITE	Shokxonestudios.com

PREFERRED MEDIUM: Mostly digital, although I still rely occasionally on pencil and paper to get a project going.

ADDITIONAL REMARKS: Some artists have said—and they aren't wrong—that nothing beats the feeling of developing your own concepts. If you can use existing popular culture as a springboard for your own creativity, as I have for much of my adult life, I believe that this can be just as much of a rush.

The Big Lebowski
18 x 24 in (46 x 61 cm)
A Poster Collective release

LOCATION
Toronto, Ontario / Canada

SITE
Ghoulishgary.com

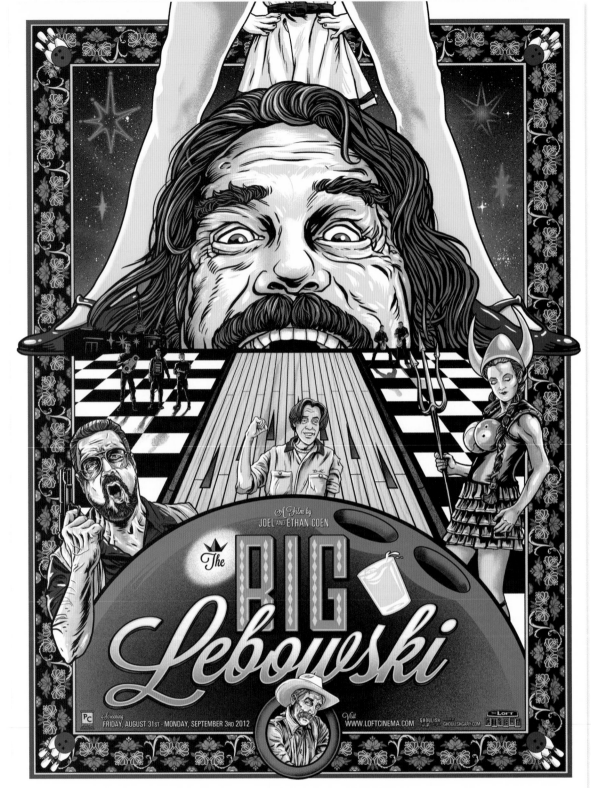

Continued from page 9

BEHIND THE POSTERS: Poster Collective requested *The Big Lebowski* and Skuzzles gave me a handful of MGM titles to choose from. *Teen Wolf* jumped out at me.

LOCATION	Toronto, Ontario / Canada
SITE	Ghoulishgary.com

Teen Wolf
24 x 36 in (61 x 91 cm)
A Skuzzles release

▶ Jason Chalker

Dr. No
12 x 18 in (30 x 46 cm)

DESIGN FIRM Manly Art

LOCATION Dallas, Texas / US

SITE Manlyart.com

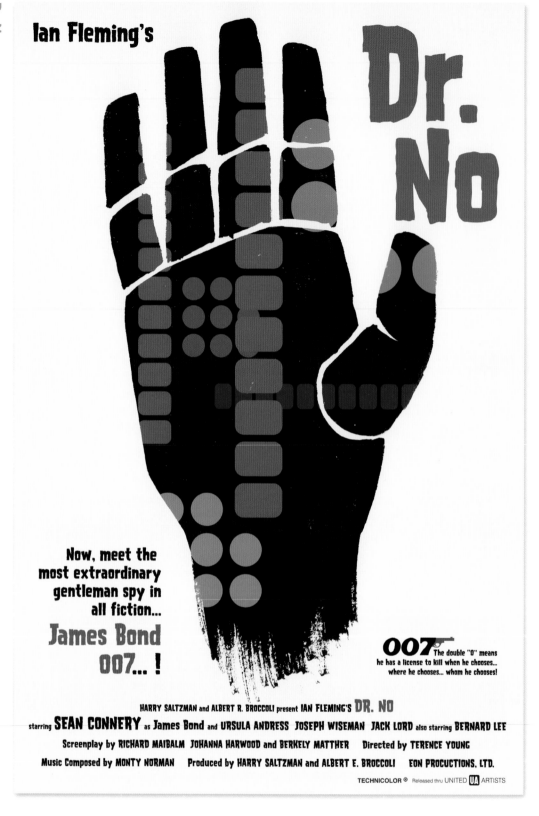

BEHIND THE POSTERS: I'm a huge fan of the Sean Connery *Bond* films. The old *Bond* films had so much style to them.

INFLUENCES: My influences are all across the board. The largest is probably the old pulp-era artists: Gil Elvgren, Ernest Chiriacka, Mort Künstler, Norm Saunders...I could keep going for a while.

Jason Chalker

DESIGN FIRM	Manly Art
LOCATION	Dallas, Texas / US
SITE	Manlyart.com

FAVORITE FILM / GENRE: That's like asking which of your children you love the most! But if I have to narrow it down, I like sci-fi/fantasy, mystery/thrillers, and spy movies.

FIRST FILM: Disney's *Robin Hood*. They did a re-release in the early '70s.
PREFERRED MEDIUM: Acrylic and ink. Most of my posters have some digital work in them. too.

Vincent Gabriele

Zombieland
18 x 24 in (46 x 61 cm)

LOCATION
Schenectady, New York / US

SITE
Behance.net/vincentgabriele
+ Etsy.com/shop/vincentgabriele

JESSE EISENBERG   WOODY HARRELSON
EMMA STONE   ABIGAIL BRESLIN

ZOMBIELAND

COLUMBIA PICTURES PRESENTS A PARIAH PRODUCTION
JESSE EISENBERG WOODY HARRELSON EMMA STONE ABIGAIL BRESLIN
WRITTEN BY RHETT REESE & PAUL WERNICK PRODUCED BY GAVIN POLONE DIRECTED BY RUBEN FLEISCHER

BEHIND THE POSTERS: I'm a big movie nerd and love graphic design, so the two were bound to merge at some point. I began creating alternate movie posters at Sage College of Albany, and *Zombieland* was one of the first that I made. *Blue Velvet* [right] came along soon thereafter.

If I enjoy a movie and think of an effective and sometimes humorous visual to represent it, I'll immediately start working on a poster. I'm drawn to the iconic and most memorable parts of a movie, and like creating a piece that captures this. So, basically, if you've seen the related movie, you will appreciate the poster, and if you haven't, you simply won't get it. This makes the viewer feel like they're in on the joke. I like that.

LOCATION Schenectady, New York / US

SITE Behance.net/vincentgabriele
+ Etsy.com/shop/vincentgabriele

DAVID LYNCH'S

BLUE VELVET

DE LAURENTIIS ENTERTAINMENT GROUP PRESENTS A DAVID LYNCH FILM
KYLE MACLACHLAN ISABELLA ROSSELLINA LAURA DERN & DENNIS HOPPER
MUSIC BY FREDERICK ELMES WRITTEN BY DAVID LYNCH DIRECTED BY DAVID LYNCH

INFLUENCES: Saul Bass is an obvious influence. He's a rock star. I'm sure his name is going to pop up a few times throughout this book for this question. His iconic and minimalist solutions to movie posters are just phenomenal.

FAVORITE FILM / GENRE: It seems like an injustice to all the great movies that I've seen to only pick one, but my go-to answer to this question always seems to be *American Beauty*. All around, it's one of the greatest movies that I've ever seen.

FIRST FILM: Classic Disney films. I might have seen *The Fox and the Hound* 30 times.

PREFERRED MEDIUM: I work almost entirely in Photoshop and, when needed, Illustrator.

ADDITIONAL REMARKS: I would love to make a career out of designing official movie posters. This book is great evidence of the popular resurgence in movie poster design and the interesting artwork that independent designers are creating. Hopefully, official movie posters will become ballsy again soon, and we can rid ourselves of the cookie cutter one-sheets.

Rushmore
14 x 22 in (35 x 55 cm)

LOCATION Ballarat, Victoria / Australia

SITE Travisprice.com.au

BEHIND THE POSTERS: I can still remember going to see *Rushmore* at the cinema back in 1998. It was the first Wes Anderson film that I had seen and was in awe of every facet of it: the cinematography, the soundtrack and music by Mark Mothersbaugh, not to mention the storyline and characters. Jason Schwartzman was so intense and Bill Murray is just awesome. It really stuck with me, and *Rushmore* made me a big Schwartzman and Anderson fan.

INFLUENCES: That's a hard one, as I am always influenced by different things at different times. However, constants would be: Directors: Wes Anderson, The Coen Brothers, Guy Ritchie, Quentin Tarantino, Jean-Pierre Jeunet. Artists/illustrators: Jamie Hewlett, Jim Phillips, Richard Allen, Ken Taylor, Nathan Jurevicius, House Industries.

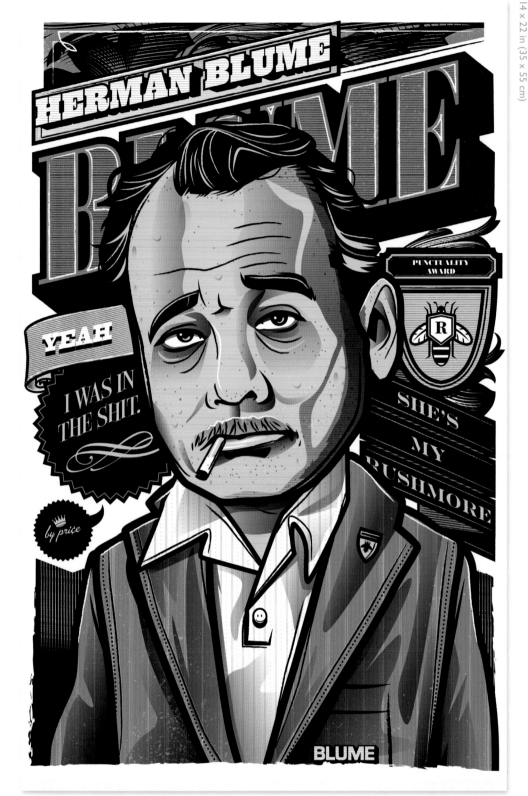

FAVORITE FILM / GENRE: My current favorite films (in no specific order) would be: *Rushmore, The Royal Tenenbaums, The Big Lebowski, O Brother Where Art Thou?, The Goonies, Stand by Me, Amélie, RocknRolla,* and *Django Unchained.*

FIRST FILM: I'm pretty sure it was *E.T.* at a drive-in theater in the back of the orange family Datsun...and think I may have cried at the end.

PREFERRED MEDIUM: Vector (digital illustration).
ADDITIONAL REMARKS: What's great about alternative film art is they are created for love, not money...and it shows!

Mark Welser

Night of the Living Dead
11 x 17 in (28 × 43 cm)

LOCATION Erie, Pennsylvania / US

SITE Etsy.com/people/swelser

THEY WON'T
STAY DEAD!

An IMAGE TEN Production

NIGHT OF THE LIVING DEAD

They keep coming back in a
bloodthirsty lust for
HUMAN FLESH!...
Pits the dead against the living
in a struggle for survival!

Starring JUDITH O'DEA DUANE JONES MARILYN EASTMAN KARL HARDMAN JUDITH RIDLEY KEITH WAYNE

Produced by Russel W. Streiner and Karl Hardman - Directed by George A. Romero - Screenplay by John A. Russo - A Walter Reade Orginization Presentation - Released by Continental

BEHIND THE POSTERS: There's a small horror fest in my town every year, so I decided that I would set up a table, later realizing that I didn't have many horror items to sell (my background is mostly in comic book-style illustration). So, I put together several horror-themed posters. I didn't think that they would have much of a life after the show was over. Turns out that people really liked them and requested additional posters. The *Ferris Bueller* design [right] was a commission from a user on Etsy, and I've done a few others as special requests as well.

INFLUENCES: Jack Kirby, Walt Simonson, Erik Larsen, etc. (comic book guys). For these posters, however, it all comes back to a Saul Bass style.
FAVORITE FILM / GENRE: *Tron.* I can never get enough of *Tron.*

Mark Welser

LOCATION Erie, Pennsylvania / US

SITE Etsy.com/people/swelser

FIRST FILM: The first movie that I was obsessed with was *The Dark Crystal*. I watched the VHS video so many times that my older brothers ran a heavy duty magnet over it (so I couldn't play it any more). Bastards.

PREFERRED MEDIUM: I prefer old fashioned hand-drawn pencil and ink. I create posters in Photoshop but only have a very basic handle on how to use the program. Enough to get by, I suppose.

More artwork from Mark Welser on pages 182 and 183

An American Werewolf in London
24 x 36 in (61 x 91 cm)

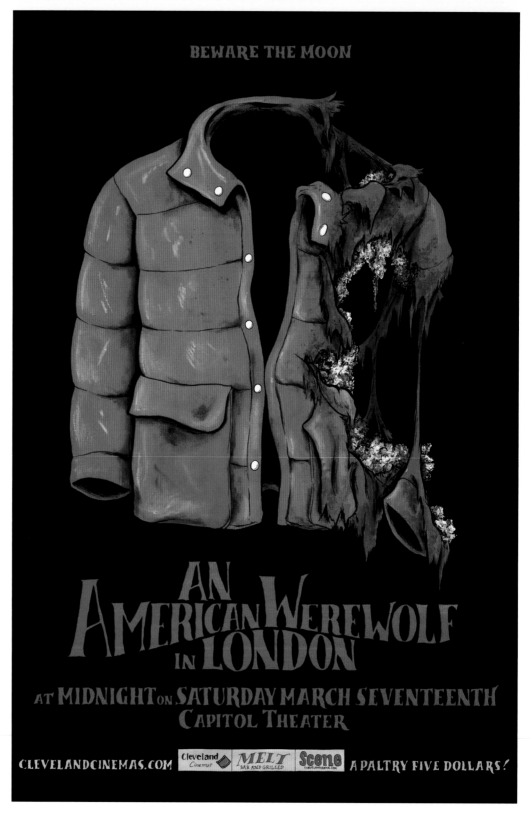

LOCATION Cleveland, Ohio / US

SITE Thelakeeriemonster.com

BEHIND THE POSTER: This poster was created for one of Cleveland Cinemas' Late Shift Movies (a midnight film series). I was a fan of *An American Werewolf in London*, although I am somewhat torn because of Landis' whole manslaughter situation [a lawsuit that stemmed from the filming of *Twilight Zone: The Movie*].

INFLUENCES: *Swamp Thing* artist John Totleben, Charles Burns, '70s schlock posters. The usual stuff.

FAVORITE FILM / GENRE: My default favorite film is *Jaws*, and horror is my default favorite genre. I'll watch almost anything, though.

FIRST FILM: John Carpenter's remake of *The Thing*. I was four or five at the time, and my dad didn't know how severe the flick was. I didn't make it past the dog kennel scene without having to be carried out of the theater in tears.

PREFERRED MEDIUM: Pen and ink.

Justin Bartlett

DESIGN FIRM VBERKVLT (Über-Cult)
LOCATION San Diego, California / US
SITE Vberkvlt.com

BEHIND THE POSTER: Originally it was for a gallery show in 2010 called "Video Violence," where the participants were asked to illustrate and/or re-design a VHS box for a '70s/'80s cult horror film. Then, in 2012, the organizers of Screamfest used it for their John Carpenter tribute (benefitting the Humane Society).

INFLUENCES: Not all of these are a direct visual influence on my work, but they are in terms of passion, drive, and vision (and some of their movies have been embedded in my psyche since I was a kid): John Carpenter, David Cronenberg, Panos Cosmatos, Ridley Scott, Steven Lisberger, Michael Mann, Nicolas Winding Refn, David Lynch, Paul Verhoeven, and Rene Laloux.

FAVORITE FILM / GENRE: Although the majority of science fiction movies are bad (since the source material is hard to dumb down and simplify for mass viewing via the Hollywood model), it's still my favorite genre and *Blade Runner* is my favorite film.
FIRST FILM: *The Muppet Movie*, when I was two.
PREFERRED MEDIUM: Rancid raven's blood on aged goat skin parchment.
ADDITIONAL REMARKS: EMBRACE VISUAL HELL!!!

Pink Flamingos / Desperate Living / Polyester / Hairspray
24 x 36 in (61 x 91 cm)
A Mondo release

DESIGNERS JW and Melissa Buchanan

LOCATION Milwaukee, Wisconsin / US

SITE Thelittlefriendsofprintmaking.com

BEHIND THE POSTER: Alamo Drafthouse was doing a series of outdoor screenings of cult films. We were lucky enough to get hired to make some posters for the series, including a festival of John Waters' films shown in the park in Baltimore where he illegally filmed much of *Pink Flamingos*. We're big John Waters fans, so we had lots of fun geeking out while drawing all the little details and outrageous bits from his films.

INFLUENCES: Cuban silkscreen film poster art of the 1960s and 1970s was a major influence for us when we were starting Little Friends, particularly the work of Eduardo Munoz Bachs.

FAVORITE FILM / GENRE: According to Netflix, we like "Depressing Documentaries" and "Mind-bending Cerebral Thrillers" (not sure if that's a thing). We've probably watched *The Big Lebowski* in excess of 200 times.

FIRST FILM: [Melissa]: The first movie that I recall seeing was *An American Werewolf in London*, which I almost certainly should not have seen at that age. I mostly remember the full-frontal male nudity.

PREFERRED MEDIUM: Silkscreen.

One Crazy Summer / Wet Hot American Summer
22 x 39 in (56 x 100 cm)

▼
Philip E. Pascuzzo

DESIGN FIRM | Pepco Studio
LOCATION | Albany, New York / US
SITE | Pepcostudio.com

BEHIND THE POSTER: Mike Keegan, the film programmer for The Roxie Theater in San Francisco, contacted me about doing a poster for a double feature. I love both films, and decided to execute the illustrations in a very minimal approach, choosing red, white, and blue since both are American summer flicks.

INFLUENCES: Paul Rand, Milton Glaser, and Seymour Chwast. I love design, art, music, and film from mid-twentieth century to the 1980s.

FAVORITE FILM / GENRE: The work of directors in the 1970s really inspire me. Robert Altman, Woody Allen, Hal Ashby, and John Cassavetes all made really amazing films during this time, ones that I can watch again and again.

FIRST FILM: I have great memories of seeing *Gremlins* in the theater for the first time. I brought my mean-tempered Stripe doll and sat there super-pumped.

PREFERRED MEDIUM: All of my work ends up digital at this point, but I still do a lot of brush-and-ink and painting in my work. I often scan in textures/sketches and fine-tune them in Photoshop.

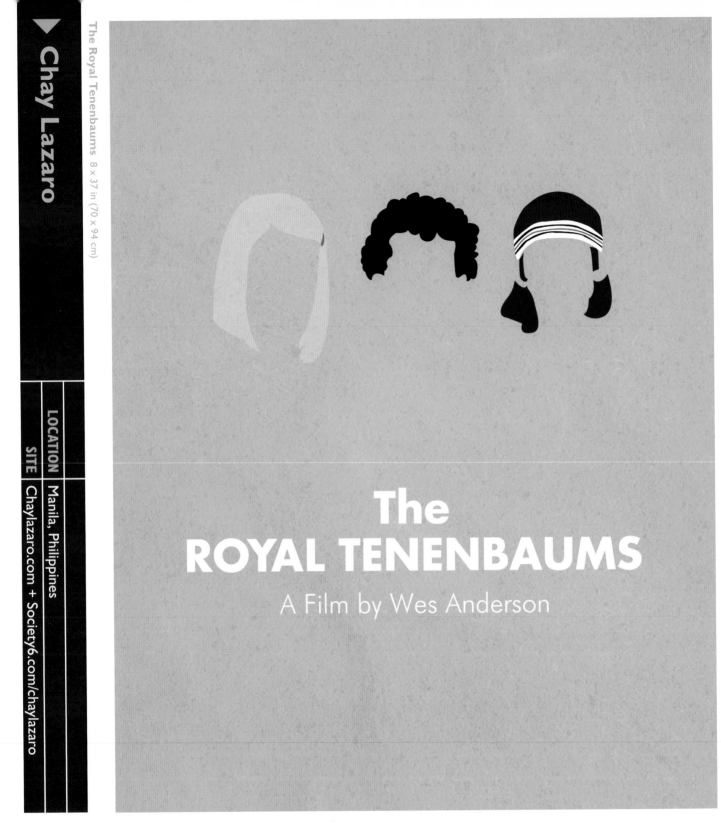

LOCATION Manila, Philippines

SITE Chaylazaro.com + Society6.com/chaylazaro

The
ROYAL TENENBAUMS
A Film by Wes Anderson

BEHIND THE POSTERS: When I watched *The Royal Tenenbaums* for the first time, the trend of creating alternative movie posters was on the rise. Both *Pretty in Pink* [right] and *The Royal Tenenbaums* have very iconic elements, and I just couldn't help but to join the bandwagon and recreate these movie posters.

INFLUENCES: Wes Anderson and his films have definitely inspired a lot of my posters.

PRETTY IN PINK
A John Hughes Production

FAVORITE FILM / GENRE: Some of my favorite films include *The Breakfast Club, Before Sunset, Jeux d'Enfants,* and *The Royal Tenenbaums,* of course. I don't really have a favorite genre, but I do go through phases where I watch films of a particular genre one after the other. Such was the case when I did the poster for *Pretty in Pink*—I was in an '80s rom-com phase.

FIRST FILM: *The Lion King.*
PREFERRED MEDIUM: Digital (Adobe Photoshop).

The Rocky Horror Picture Show
18 × 24 in (46 × 61 cm)
A Poster Collective release

LOCATION Woodstock, Maryland / US

SITE Joshuabudich.com

BEHIND THE POSTERS: *Rocky Horror* was a commission for Poster Collective. It was the first print in a new series for movie showings at The Loft Cinema [Tucson, Arizona]. *Life Aquatic* [right] was my contribution to Spoke Art's annual "Bad Dads: A Tribute to Wes Anderson" art show. *Life Aquatic* is one of my all-time favorites, and my personal fave of Wes Anderson's films.

INFLUENCES: My art is most heavily influenced by my love of comic book artists: Larsen, McFarlane, Lee, Bisley, Mignola, just to name a few. Film-wise: Wes Anderson, Ridley Scott, Coppola, Spielberg, Lucas, Fincher.

FAVORITE FILM / GENRE: I'd be doing myself an injustice to not admit my love affair with *Star Wars* (OT: check out my *Star Wars* collection at Joshuabudich.com/SWCollection). In general I like sci-fi, comedy, and foreign/artsy-fartsy, and my favorite films include *Alien, The Terminator, Anchorman, The City of Lost Children, Delicatessen,* and *The Princess Bride.*

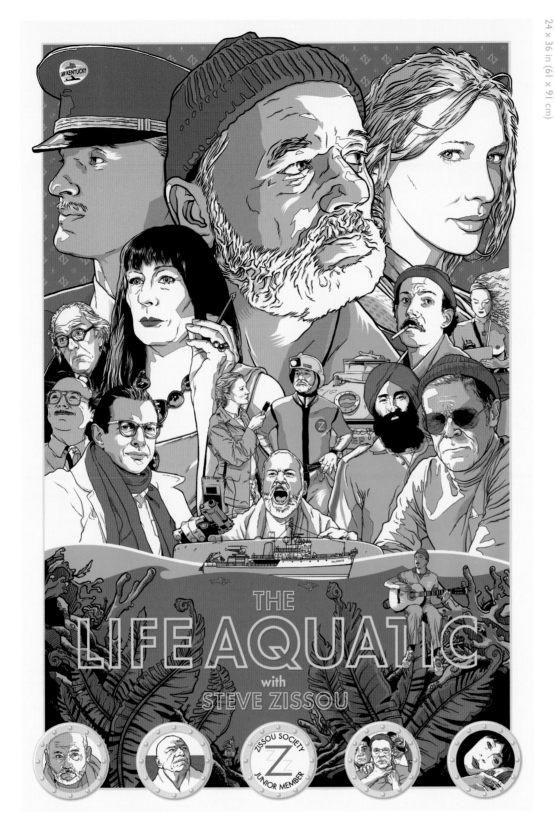

The Life Aquatic with Steve Zissou
24 x 36 in (61 x 91 cm)

LOCATION Woodstock, Maryland / US
SITE Joshuabudich.com

FIRST FILM: *The Empire Strikes Back.*
PREFERRED MEDIUM: I love to work with pen and ink, and digitally with a Wacom tablet. I mainly create screen prints and giclées.

ADDITIONAL REMARKS: I live in the DC/Baltimore area with my wife, 4-year-old son, and our Scottish Terrier. I've been working the screen print game for over five years, producing work for galleries (Spoke Art, Gallery 1988, Blunt Graffix), and various independent commissions for editorial and corporate entities (*SI Kids Magazine*, Team GB - 2012 Olympic Games, *NASCAR Illustrated Magazine*). I like to brew my own beer, grind my own meat, and grow my own veggies.

BEHIND THE POSTERS: When I'm designing a neon movie sign, I try to choose a film that would possibly use a promotional neon sign outside the cinema. *Pulp Fiction* and *Pee-Wee's Big Adventure* [right] are both favorite films of mine and seemed to fit the bill. Also, creating a neon sign requires an animation that loops, so dance moves are ideal subject matter and both *Pulp Fiction* and *Pee-Wee's Big Adventure* have iconic dance scenes.

INFLUENCES: Chuck Jones and Hitchcock are heroes of mine, incredibly influential directors in their own fields. I also love the amazing art of Noma Bar. He has a great line and his minimalist portraits are beautifully drawn.

FAVORITE FILM / GENRE: Hitchcock's *Rear Window* is my favorite film. I watch it at least once a year and I always discover something new each time. It's pure visual cinema. You can turn the sound down and still understand every beat of the story.

FIRST FILM: My parents took me to see *The Jungle Book* when I was five years old and I was blown away by the animation. I can remember sitting in awe and even chastising my mother for laughing. "What's so funny about the dancing bear? Look at the amazing artistry mum!" It was a huge inspiration and I still consider the character animation to be some of the finest ever.

LOCATION Manchester / UK

SITE Mrwhaite.com

PREFERRED MEDIUM: My training is in traditional 2-D animation, and it's only relatively recently that I made the move to digital. I'm now completely sold on it and I use Flash to design my neon work. The ability to fine tune my animation as I work and also draw with glowing lines makes the whole process much more enjoyable.

ADDITIONAL REMARKS: My first attempt at neon was a *Ghostbusters* sign complete with flashing proton streams and a struggling Slimer. Someone recently sent me a photo taken in a Mexican restaurant in Australia where they had a real neon version of this design on the wall. I'm still not sure what the *Ghostbusters/ Mexico* link is but I was impressed all the same!

Deep Throat
28 × 40 in (70 × 102 cm)

BEHIND THE POSTER: After seeing so many minimalist posters, I thought that I would give it a try. I came across the original *Deep Throat* poster and it was already close to being a minimalist poster, yet it was terrible. Nevertheless, the film made a ton of money and became the most famous porn film of all time. I gave it about as much time as the original designer put into it, and came up with this in about 20 minutes.

FAVORITE FILM / GENRE: *Jaws.* My mom took my cousin and I to see it in the summer of '75. I was never the same after. I thought about that movie day and night for months. I would draw the shark from the poster on anything that I could find—on loose leaf paper, on school books, in the sand. I've seen it well over a hundred times and watch it every summer.

FIRST FILM: Likely a Disney movie. However, I would beg my parents to take me to see "grown-up movies" like *The Poseidon Adventure.* When *Earthquake* came out (in Sensurround!) I drove my parents insane until they finally relented.

RUSS MEYER

Faster, PUSSYCAT! KILL! KILL!

TURA SATANA   HAJI   LORI WILLIAMS   SUSAN BERNARD
STUART LANCASTER   PAUL TRINKA   DENNIS BUSCH   RAY BARLOW   MICKEY FOXX

Faster, Pussycat! Kill! Kill!
20 × 28 in (50 × 70 cm - B2)

Andrea Gallo

ALIAS   roosterization

LOCATION   Italy

SITE   Behance.net/andreagallo
+ Flickr.com/photos/roosterization/

BEHIND THE POSTER: I've always liked Russ Meyer's movies and wanted to represent each of his films with a simple icon or pictogram. I chose to use a pair of boobs since they are easily recognizable as two semicircles. I then started to differentiate the various posters for this series [*Faster Pussycat* is one poster from a series of six] based on clothing of the protagonists in his films.

INFLUENCES: I grew up with Bruno Munari, a designer and Italian artist. Concerning graphic design I really like the Swiss school, in particular artists such as Richard P. Lohse, Hans Neuburg, and Max Huber. In the field of cinema I definitely took a lot of inspiration from Saul Bass. His pieces were so linear and clean.

PREFERRED MEDIUM: I usually keep a little notebook in every jacket for developing ideas. Sometimes I enjoy scanning pieces of notebook and stacking them with old works to see what happens. I normally use Illustrator, Photoshop, and other Adobe software to finish the process.

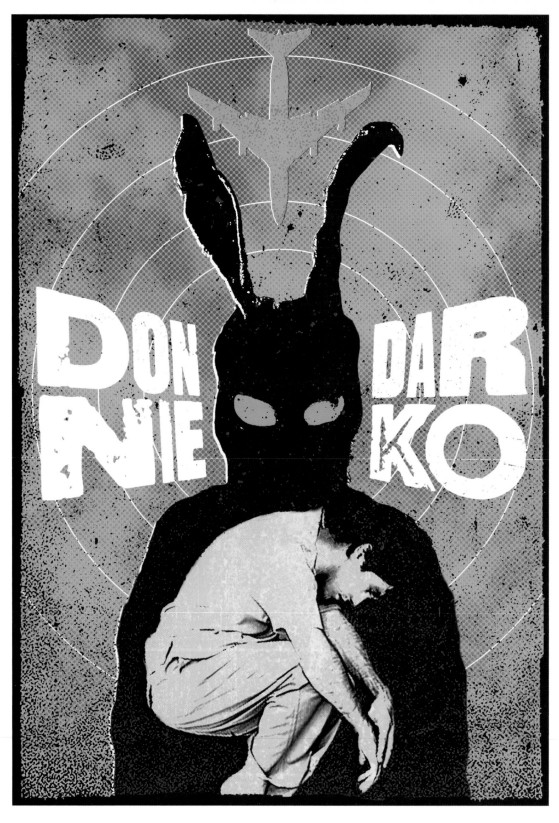

BEHIND THE POSTERS: *Donnie Darko* and *Mulholland Drive* [right] are favorites that I've watched countless times. Richard Kelly and David Lynch are experts at crafting self-contained universes run by a believable—if not always comprehensible—dream logic.

I approached both directors' movies by letting go of traditional narrative rules and allowing emotional dynamics to tell the story on a subconscious level. Some people have problems with the impressionistic nature of these films. The minds of troubled teens and guilt-ridden spurned lovers typically aren't clear and rational, and I think that these movies reflect that successfully.

Both also have Moebius strip timelines that somehow simultaneously illuminate and confound their audiences more with each viewing. I love hearing all of the varied and contradictory interpretations, and find my own opinions continually evolving. I can't say that about many straightforward films that I watch once and forget.

INFLUENCES: I'm hooked by strong iconic visual metaphors. I also favor bold vision and experimentation over perfection. In addition to Richard Kelly and David Lynch, I'm a fan of Guy Maddin, Terry Gilliam, Jean-Pierre Jeunet, Hiroshi Teshigahara, and Luis Buñuel. Artists who I love include Steven Cerio, Junko Mizuno, Gary Panter, Yoko D'Holbachie, and Matthieu Bessudo (aka McBess).

Mike Langlie

LOCATION Boston, Massachusetts / US

SITE Yipyop.com

FAVORITE FILM / GENRE: It's a tie between *The American Astronaut* and *The Forbidden Zone*. Both fearlessly incorporate almost every imaginable genre.

FIRST FILM: The first film that I dragged my parents to was *Time Bandits*. It's also the first film that I dragged my parents back to.

PREFERRED MEDIUM: I dabble in illustration, design, music, writing, and even a bit of admittedly bad acting. But my dream would be to work in film. It mixes many separate crafts into something so much larger and alive. When done well, it's beautiful and intimidating.

ADDITIONAL REMARKS: Good art inspires others to create something themselves. A good film makes people want to explore and extend their view of the world, such as fan-made posters, fiction, comics, and even cosplay. I see those tributes as a dialog among fans that enriches the experience, rather than as a copyright risk (as some studios consider them).

Friday the 13th Part III
11 x 16 in (28 x 41 cm)

LOCATION Lakewood, Ohio / US

SITE Chodartist.com

BEHIND THE POSTERS: I love both of these flicks, and have posters for them hanging in my bedroom. *Friday the 13th Part III* is definitely my favorite out of the *Friday the 13th* series. There are not many things cooler than seeing it in 3-D on the big screen. And *Fight Club* [right] is, hands down, the best film ever made. From the story to the cinematography to the score. Everything is near perfect. Also, I don't think that there is a movie that has affected my outlook on the world as much as *Fight Club*. All hail David Fincher.

INFLUENCES: I am influenced largely by comic book artists. My favorites are Paul Pope, Ashley Wood, Jae Lee, Kent Williams, Dave McKean, Chris Bachalo, Travis Charest, James Jean, Eric Canete, Geof Darrow, Jason Pearson, Mike Mignola, Becky Cloonan, and Fabio Moon.

I also love the work of Egon Schiele, Gustav Klimt, Alfons Mucha, and Henri de Toulouse-Lautrec.

Fight Club
27 × 40 in (69 × 102 cm)

▶ **Chod**

LOCATION Lakewood, Ohio / US

SITE Chodartist.com

Plus, I am heavily influenced by film directors. Directing would definitely be my dream job. Favorites include David Fincher, Darren Aronofsky, Baz Luhrmann, Quentin Tarantino, old school John Carpenter, Dario Argento, Takashi Miike, Guy Ritchie, Paul Thomas Anderson, David Cronenberg, Alfred Hitchcock, Hayao Miyazaki, Genndy Tartakovsky, Sam Raimi, Brad Bird, and Tim Burton.

FAVORITE FILM / GENRE: Horror. Horror films are either scary, gory, funny, or so bad that they become funny.

FIRST FILM: *The Muppet Movie* at the drive-in theater with my family.

PREFERRED MEDIUM: I mostly work with acrylic paint and ink. Sometimes I throw in some collage material or other mixed media to keep from getting bored. I also work with digital coloring over inked pieces every once in a while.

ADDITIONAL REMARKS: I want to give props to Breakneck Gallery and The Pop Shop Gallery [both in Lakewood, Ohio] for hosting the Cinematic Redux Art Shows that I curated. Both were alternative movie poster art shows. And also to Cleveland Cinemas for giving me the opportunity to create posters for some of their special events.

LOCATION Melbourne, Victoria / Australia

SITE Heathkillen.com

Continued from page 32

A Clockwork Orange
17 x 23 in (42 x 59 cm - A2)

LOCATION Melbourne, Victoria / Australia

SITE Heathkillen.com

BEHIND THE POSTER: I was seeing a lot of alternative movie posters online, but noticed that films were being repeated, so my aim was to pick a film that hadn't been recreated as much. *Almost Famous* came to me straight away. I'm a music enthusiast, especially music of the '70s, and have seen this film several times.

INFLUENCES: I love the illustrations of Stanley Chow, I'm a huge fan of Pixar, and Andy Warhol's work is timeless and always relevant.

FAVORITE FILM / GENRE: My favorite film is *Amélie*. It encompasses everything that I enjoy in films—a lovely story, witty lines, a beautiful setting, an amazing soundtrack, gorgeous cinematography, and a great title sequence/end credits. I also enjoy films by Woody Allen. His dialogue is fantastic.

FIRST FILM: *The Aristocats*. I think it was re-released in cinemas in the early '90s, so I would have been six or seven.

PREFERRED MEDIUM: Adobe Illustrator.

ADDITIONAL REMARKS: I love film! I hope to design more posters in the future. It's nice to be creative with something that you love.

TOP FIVE RECORDS

(23735) **33M** TFR·02

•**HIGH FIDELITY**•

BEHIND THE POSTER: *High Fidelity* has always been one of my top five films. The movie strikes the perfect balance of comedy, drama, pop culture, and romance (or lack thereof). So, I was working on illustration ideas for a magazine article and ended up with a tiny thumbnail sketch of a heart shaped vinyl record. I immediately made the connection to *High Fidelity* and decided to also make a poster.

INFLUENCES: I take a lot of inspiration from the 1950s—whether it's a piece of animation, character design, or a terrible sci-fi B movie.

FIRST FILM: My younger brother and I went to see the *Super Mario Bros.* movie. We sat down expecting it to be as brilliant as, if not better than, the video game. After twenty minutes we realized that it was a terrible waste of time and decided to sneak into *The Last Action Hero*. It was a far more enjoyable experience.

PREFERRED MEDIUM: I tend to work with pencil, ink, paper, and a scalpel. I make a mess and then scan everything into my computer, where I assemble the image and color it digitally.

Tim Doyle

The Transformers: The Movie
16 x 24 in (41 x 61 cm)

DESIGN FIRM Nakatomi Inc.

LOCATION Austin, Texas / US

SITE Mrdoyle.com + Nakatomiinc.com

BEHIND THE POSTERS: I'm a huge fan of both *Robocop* and the animated 1985 *Transformers* movie (not the Michael Bay abortions). I was lucky enough to be commissioned by movie theaters to produce those prints for them.

INFLUENCES: Right now I'm really grooving on Tomer Hanuka, Moebius, and Geof Darrow. As far as filmmakers go, I'm always going to be influenced by David Lynch and Stanley Kubrick, even if it's not entirely evident in my art.

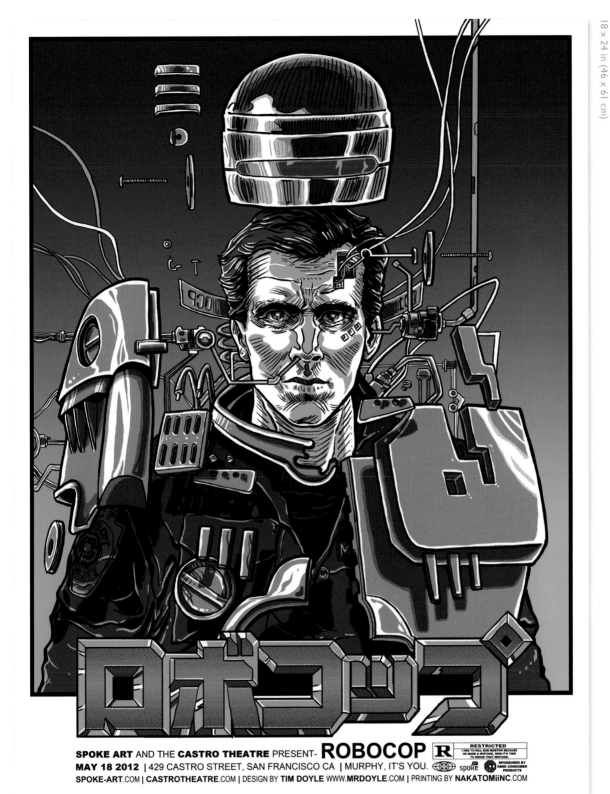

RoboCop
18 x 24 in (46 x 61 cm)

Tim Doyle

DESIGN FIRM	Nakatomi Inc.
LOCATION	Austin, Texas / US
SITE	Mrdoyle.com + Nakatomiinc.com

SPOKE ART AND THE CASTRO THEATRE PRESENT- ROBOCOP **R** **RESTRICTED** I HAD TO KILL BOB MORTON BECAUSE HE MADE A MISTAKE, NOW IT'S TIME TO ERASE THAT MISTAKE.

MAY 18 2012 | 429 CASTRO STREET, SAN FRANCISCO CA | MURPHY, IT'S YOU. SPONSORED BY OMNI CONSUMER PRODUCTS

SPOKE-ART.COM | CASTROTHEATRE.COM | DESIGN BY TIM DOYLE WWW.MRDOYLE.COM | PRINTING BY NAKATOMiiNC.COM

FAVORITE FILM / GENRE: My top five favorite films, in no particular order, are *Robocop, Pee-Wee's Big Adventure, Blade Runner, Raising Arizona,* and *Babe 2: Pig in the City.* Infinitely watchable and enjoyable. Now, I know there are better films, but as much as I might love *Mulholland Drive* with every fiber of my being, it's not something I could watch over and over again.

FIRST FILM: Probably *Condorman* or *Tron.* Those made a big impact on my little brain. But the first film I saw, according to my parents, was *The Muppet Movie.*

PREFERRED MEDIUM: Pen and ink, with a follow-through to screen printing!

Mean Streets
18 x 24 in (46 x 61 cm)

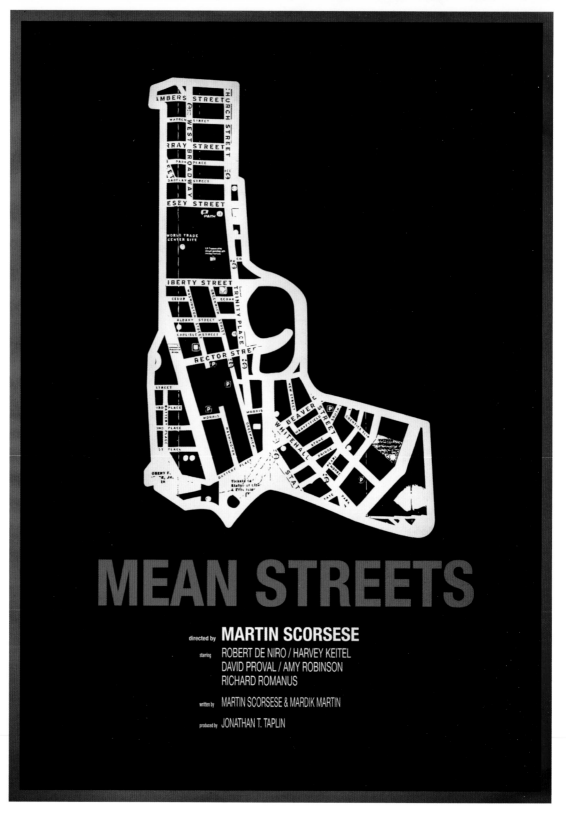

ALIAS Raid71

LOCATION Darwen / UK

SITE Raid71.com

Continued from page 13

More artwork from Chris Thornley on page 150

BEHIND THE POSTER: The first poster that I ever designed was *Mean Streets*. A local cinema had a special screening and wanted a poster to advertise it. Afterwards, I posted the image online and people started e-mailing me about its availability, which convinced me to print it.

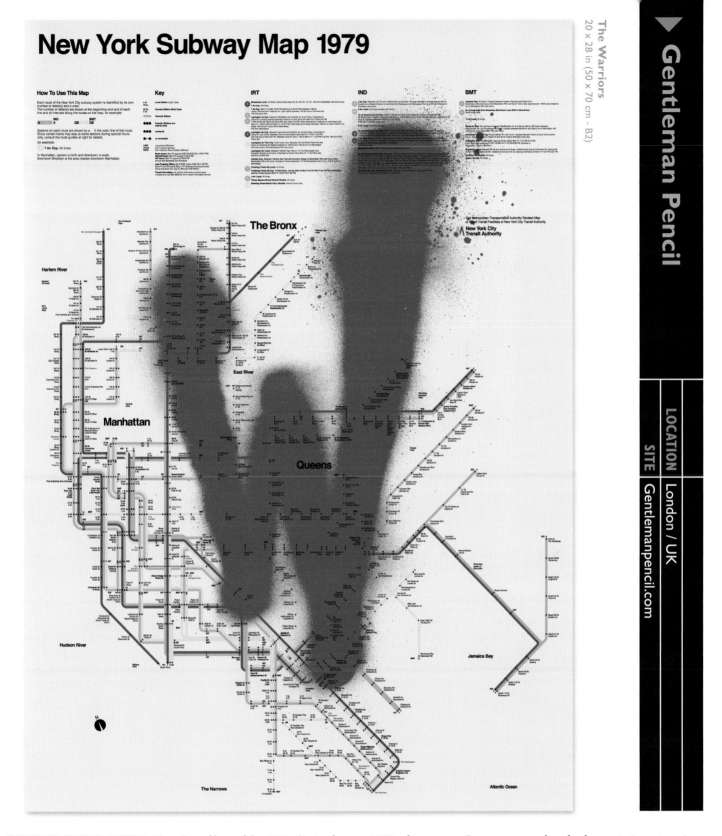

New York Subway Map 1979

The Warriors
20 x 28 in (50 x 70 cm - B2)

LOCATION	London / UK
SITE	Gentlemanpencil.com

BEHIND THE POSTER: I love how films of the 1970s (*Saturday Night Fever*, *Escape from New York*, *Rocky*) painted American cities in such a dark and desolate light, and *The Warriors* is an extension of this. Dark, dirty, scary New York—a million miles from how the city is portrayed today.

Not wanting this to be a film poster in the traditional sense, I brought together the themes of flight and territory while creating something that sat snugly between artifact from the film and a piece of design. I wasn't able to find a decent copy of a NY map, so I painstakingly recreated it from a jpeg of Vignelli's original 1972 subway map. Gang names replaced subway stations at various points across the different metro lines to trace The Warriors' journey through rival turf as they bop all the way back to Coney.

FAVORITE FILM / GENRE: The ones that I can watch repeatedly without getting bored are *The Warriors*, *Blade Runner*, *Alien*, and *Gattaca*.

FIRST FILM: I think that would be my dad sneaking me into *The Living Daylights* when I was four.

PREFERRED MEDIUM: Digital. I can fiddle with it as much as I want and still keep it clean.

Dimitri Simakis

Mac and Me
11 x 17 in (28 x 43 cm)

DESIGN FIRM Valiant Effort Studios / Everything Is Terrible!

LOCATION Los Angeles, California / US

SITE Valianteffort.net + Everythingisterrible.com

BEHIND THE POSTERS: *Mac and Me* might be the greatest American kids' movie of its time, and here's why: It's not the slightest bit apologetic that it's a huge *E.T.* rip-off, and that takes balls. You can tell the studio didn't give a shit how fucked up it was, just as long as it had at least one brown alien, some dancing, and lots and lots of hamburgers. It's more of a commercial for McDonald's and Coke than anything else. And let's be honest—the only way to really enjoy it is with the company of others. If you watch this movie alone, you might be a creep. Anyway, this movie is a party I'd like to be invited to forever and ever.

20,000 Leagues Under the Sea—I couldn't imagine more of a dream poster for me to create. Stephin Merritt is my musical hero, and The Cinefamily here in Los Angeles is the greatest movie theater that ever will be —and I am so happy to be a programmer there. Plus, a live score like this comes once in a lifetime, so I hope I captured the event nicely. Of course the film/score blew us all away that night, and I am proud to say that the only thing Mr. Merritt has ever said to me was "but there's no octopus in the movie" after I meekly gave him a poster. In my defense there is an octopus on the original poster, but what was I going to do, argue? The man is ABBA, Brian Wilson, Jesus and Mary Chain, and New Order all wrapped up in one sarcastic package!

20,000 Leagues Under the Sea
27 x 40 in (69 x 102 cm)

DESIGN FIRM Valiant Effort Studios / Everything Is Terrible!
LOCATION Los Angeles, California / US
SITE Valianteffort.net + Everythingisterrible.com

INFLUENCES: Jim Henson, '80s action films, video logo intros, *Jurassic Park*, Saul Bass, Fleischer cartoons, Joel Hodgson, Rob Schrab, and so many others.

FAVORITE FILM / GENRE: Fucked up kids' movies.

FIRST FILM: Either *E.T.* or *The Neverending Story* at the now defunct Broadview Theater (in Cleveland, Ohio). If I were a rich man I would rebuild that place brick by brick.

PREFERRED MEDIUM: Illustrator, Photoshop, a Wacom tablet, foam, fur, an exacto blade, and a glue gun. Screen printing is also the greatest.

ADDITIONAL REMARKS: Never be bored and never stop working on creative stuff or you might die. Life is terrifying, so keep busy making art. And check out *Everything Is Terrible!*

The Nightmare Before Christmas
28 x 32 in (71 x 81 cm)

LOCATION Catalunya / Spain

SITE Joelamatguell.com

BEHIND THE POSTER: I began making film art as part of a final school project that consisted of 40 different movie posters.
INFLUENCES: I love all of the films from Tarantino, Nolan, Bong Joon Ho, and more. When it comes to art and the concepts for film posters, Olly Moss has been a huge influence.
FAVORITE FILM / GENRE: I simply love movies that deliver a strong message, or that have great dialogue (like Guy Ritchie's and Tarantino's films). I also love the *Jackass* movies. OK, so there's no message with those, but they made me laugh my ass off.

FIRST FILM: *Conan the Barbarian*. I was around six and found it at my grandma's house. I loved it.
PREFERRED MEDIUM: I like digital for the posters, especially Photoshop and Illustrator, but I also love to mix other mediums like inks and watercolors with digital.

More artwork from Joel Amat Güell on page 166

Piotr Miśkiewicz

LOCATION Łódź / Poland

SITE Drmierzwiak.deviantart.com + Plakaty.blox.pl

BEHIND THE POSTER: Gore Verbinski's version of *The Ring* is one of my favorite films. When I create a poster I try to find the simplest image that contains critical elements of the film's story, while at the same time trying to keep it visually fresh.

INFLUENCES: Other poster artists are a great source of inspiration, such as Tomasz Opasiński, Neil Kellerhouse, and Olly Moss. However, the absolute master, was, is, and always will be, the brilliant Drew Struzan. When it comes to directors, David Fincher, Michael Mann, and Quentin Tarantino top my list.

FAVORITE FILM / GENRE: Sci-fi. My favorite films include *Heat, Batman Returns, Se7en, Collateral, Children of Men, Kill Bill: Volume 1, Jackie Brown, Inglourious Basterds, Jurassic Park, Alien, Aliens, Alien 3* (extended cut), the original *Star Wars* trilogy, *The Terminator, Terminator 2,* and many others.

PREFERRED MEDIUM: Digital art.

Little Miss Sunshine
29 x 40 in (74 x 102 cm)

A FILM BY DAYTON AND FARIS

LITTLE MISS SUNSHINE

"Everybody just pretend to be normal"

Vince

BEHIND THE POSTERS: My whole collection (over 150 pieces) started out of curiosity. I routinely asked myself "What would the minimal poster look like?" when seeing any movie. Well, that spiraled out of control, and this is now more or less an addiction.

INFLUENCES: Dick Bruna is my main inspiration, best known for his children's book character Nijntje (Miffy in English). He is a Dutch graphic designer that made *Zwarte Beertjes* (*Black Bears*) book covers in the '70s. They were cheap paperbacks. He made 1,800 (!) of these covers, most of them brilliant.

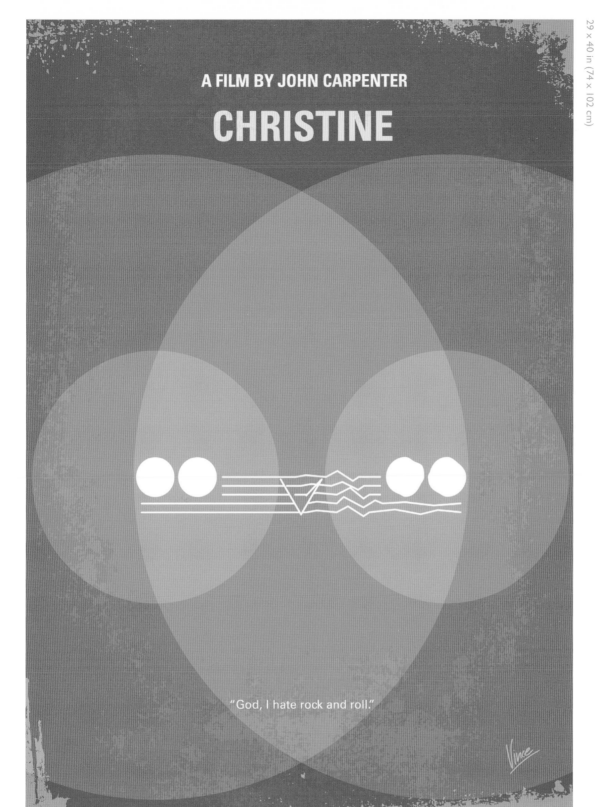

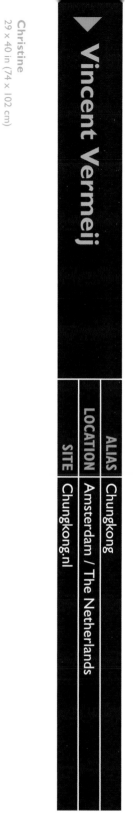

ALIAS	Chungkong
LOCATION	Amsterdam / The Netherlands
SITE	Chungkong.nl

FAVORITE FILM / GENRE: Anything by Kubrick and Tarantino.   **PREFERRED MEDIUM:** Digital.

ALIAS	Cynic with a Pencil
LOCATION	New York, New York / US
SITE	Cynicwithapencil.blogspot.com + Cynicwithapencil.tumblr.com

BEHIND THE POSTERS: *The Goonies* and *Ghostbusters* pieces were part of a themed show. A close friend and fellow illustrator, Joe Game (aka Chogrin [page 90]), invited me to participate with a group called The Autumn Society for the show, which was held at Gallery 1988. The show was called "3G" and each artist created pieces based around *The Goonies*, *Ghostbusters*, and *Gremlins*.

The Goonies and *Ghostbusters* hold a special place in my heart. I remember being about five years old and watching them over and over again until I remembered most, if not all of the lines and jokes. I'm surprised that my parents had the patience for allowing my brothers and I to loop the same films all of the time.

ALIAS	Cynic with a Pencil
LOCATION	New York, New York / US
SITE	Cynicwithapencil.blogspot.com + Cynicwithapencil.tumblr.com

INFLUENCES: Kevin Dart, Chris Reccardi, Derek Yaniger, Shane Glines, Bill Presing, Mary Blair, anything from the UPA animation style era and '50s–'60s advertising.
FAVORITE FILM / GENRE: I'm really into animation, comedy, horror, and sci-fi films. Also, almost anything from the '80s.
FIRST FILM: *Terminator 2*. My dad's awesome.

PREFERRED MEDIUM: Digital.
ADDITIONAL REMARKS: I'll keep drawing as long as people keep showing interest in my work. I'd like to thank everyone who continues to support what I love to do!

More artwork from Bobby O'Herlihy on pages 190 and 191

Straw Dogs
27 × 40 in (69 × 102 cm)

LOCATION Indianapolis, Indiana / US

SITE Josheckert.com

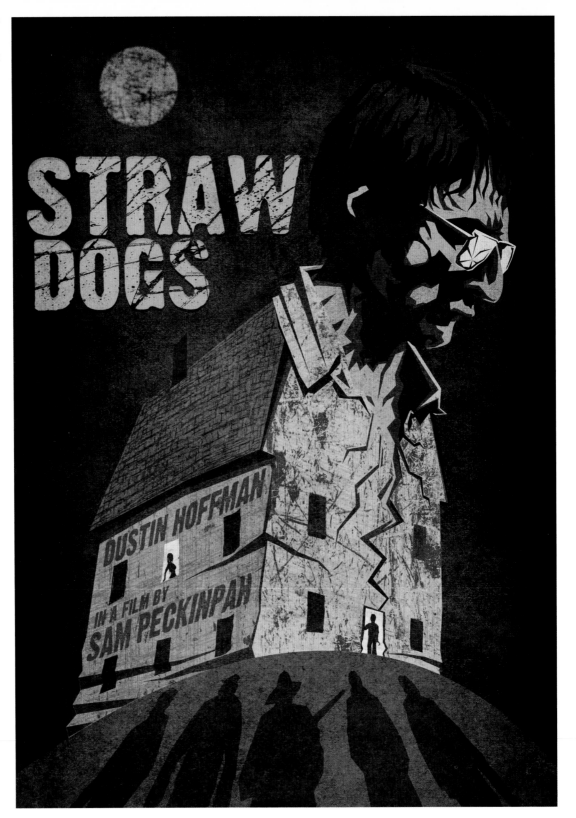

BEHIND THE POSTER: *Straw Dogs* is one of my all-time favorite films, though admittedly, as I get older it gets more and more difficult to watch. There's a brief shot toward the end of the movie in which Dustin Hoffman stands slumped over the body of one of the men he's just killed, and he doesn't look triumphant, just sad and sweaty and bloody. The way he stood there really struck me and the idea for the poster came to mind. I modeled his look in the poster after that exact shot.

INFLUENCES: The recent wave of alternative poster designers have been the biggest influence. Olly Moss, Daniel Danger, Kevin Tong, Tyler Stout, to name only a few.

FAVORITE FILM / GENRE: The entire Coen Brothers' filmography. Their style is almost a genre unto itself.
FIRST FILM: *The Wizard of Oz.* The tornado in that movie still gives me the creeps.
ADDITIONAL REMARKS: It's an honor to be featured in this book alongside so many other great artists and designers. Here's hoping the alternative poster "movement" (if we can call it that) actually has some influence on mainstream poster design.

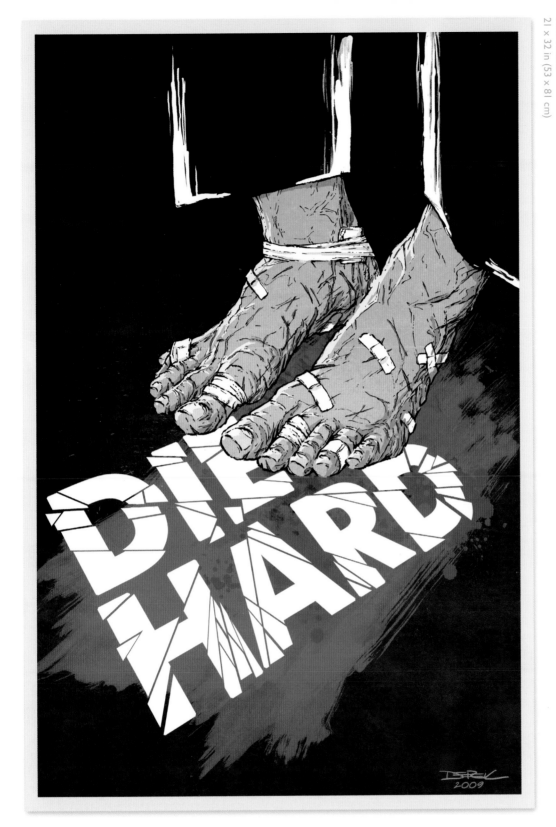

Die Hard
21 x 32 in (53 x 81 cm)

Derek Chatwood

LOCATION Seattle, Washington / US

SITE Poprelics.com

BEHIND THE POSTER: I am a big fan of *Die Hard*, especially the (at the time) original notion of an "everyman" getting the crap kicked out of him while both surviving impossible odds, and stubbornly refusing to give up. I wanted to do an illustration that focused on that vulnerability and attitude, a single image that any fan of the film would immediately understand. Plus, I wanted to practice drawing feet, which I normally suck at.

INFLUENCES: I learned how to draw from comic books, so my main influences were comic book artists, including Jean Giraud (Moebius), Frank Quietely, Geof Darrow, and Steve Epting.

FAVORITE FILM / GENRE: I'm all over the place, with the possible exception of romantic comedies and period dramas.
FIRST FILM: *Doc Savage*. I'm still afraid of green ghost snakes. Glad that never became a trend.
PREFERRED MEDIUM: I straddle between digital and meat space, drawing with pencil or ink on smooth bristol, and then scanning and painting the line in Photoshop. I like the freedom of digital (with its endless undoes), but the tactile feel of pen to paper has yet to be improved upon.

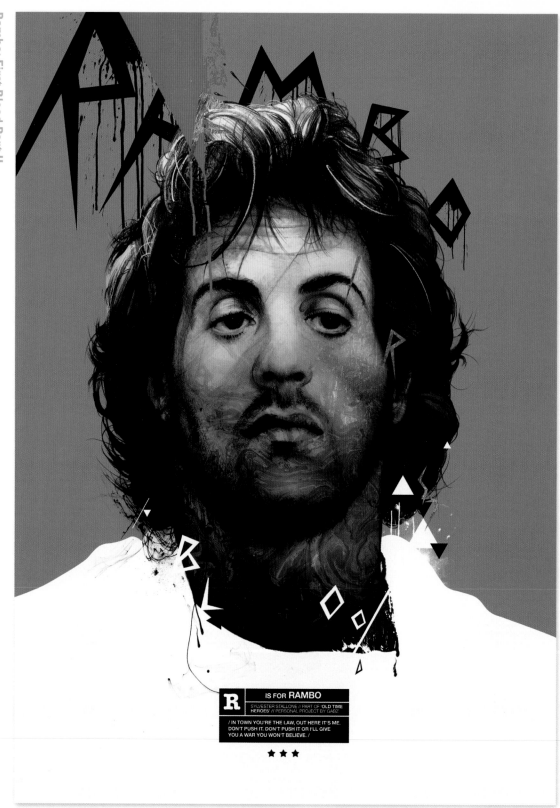

ALIAS	Gabz
LOCATION	Poznań / Poland
SITE	Iamgabz.com

R IS FOR **RAMBO**

SYLVESTER STALLONE // PART OF 'OLD TIME
HEROES' // PERSONAL PROJECT BY GABZ

/ IN TOWN YOU'RE THE LAW, OUT HERE IT'S ME.
DON'T PUSH IT. DON'T PUSH IT OR I'LL GIVE
YOU A WAR YOU WON'T BELIEVE. /

★ ★ ★

BEHIND THE POSTERS: I dig the "one man army" concept. Plus I always wanted to pay a tribute to my favorite action movie stars. Sly and Arnie were my first picks, but the plan was to also illustrate Bruce Willis, Van Damme, Chuck Norris, and so many more. Bear in mind that this was back in 2009, way before *The Expendables* stole the whole buzz.

INFLUENCES: Martin Ansin and Tyler Stout are definitely two poster artists who I look up to. I love movies in general, so naming all that inspire me is pointless, but here are a few directors who I consider personal heroes: Francis Ford Coppola, Miloš Forman, Coen Brothers, Ridley Scott, Paul Thomas Anderson, and Christopher Nolan. Huge respect!

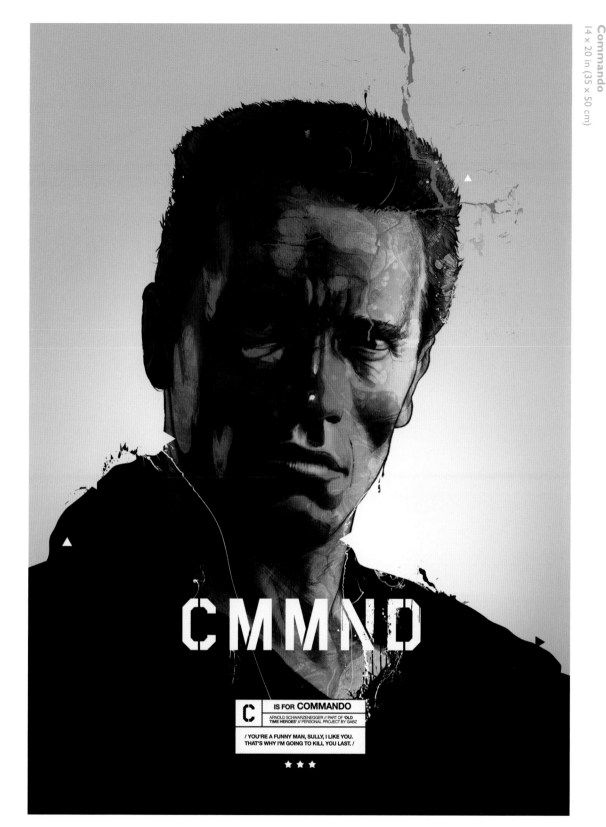

Commando
14 x 20 in (35 x 50 cm)

Grzegorz Domaradzki

ALIAS	Gabz
LOCATION	Poznań / Poland
SITE	Iamgabz.com

FAVORITE FILM / GENRE: Drama. But this doesn't mean that I don't enjoy war movies (including action films), science fiction, and even horror.
FIRST FILM: *Raiders of the Lost Ark*. Not exactly sure if it was the very first, but definitely the one that I remember.

PREFERRED MEDIUM: I enjoy pencils a lot, later remastered in Photoshop. But I also work with tablets, creating fully digital artworks using the lasso tool in Photoshop (works great for screen printing).

Superbad
12 × 18 in (30 × 46 cm)

DESIGN FIRM Bandito Design Co.
LOCATION Columbus, Ohio / US
SITE Banditodesignco.com

BEHIND THE POSTERS: Both posters were created for tribute art shows at Gallery 1988 (one for *Wet Hot American Summer*, and one for a general tribute to Judd Apatow). I am a huge fan of both flicks and confident that I could easily watch either of them every day if I had to.

INFLUENCES: Designers: Saul Bass, Charley Harper, Paul Rand. Directors: Stanley Kubrick, Sam Raimi, John Carpenter.

Ryan Brinkerhoff

DESIGN FIRM	Bandito Design Co.
LOCATION	Columbus, Ohio / US
SITE	Banditodesignco.com

FAVORITE FILM / GENRE: Horror.
FIRST FILM: Disney's *Pinocchio*.

PREFERRED MEDIUM: Silkscreen.

Leaving Las Vegas

A film by Mike Figgis

Starring Nicolas Cage Elisabeth Shue Julian Sands Richard Lewis
Steven Weber Kim Adams Emily Procter Stuart Regen Valeria Golino

Continued from page 12

More artwork from Viktor Hertz on pages 89 and 134

BEHIND THE POSTERS: Both *Magnolia* [right] and *Leaving Las Vegas* are part of my "pictogram movie posters," which was a project that summarized movies in a single, or just a few, pictograms. My first in this series was *Psycho*, and then I kept going. There are a total of 31 posters to date, and there might be a continuation of these sometime in the future.

Magnolia

A film by Paul Thomas Anderson

Starring Julianne Moore William H. Macy John C. Reilly Tom Cruise Philip Baker Hall
Philip Seymour Hoffman Jason Robards Alfred Molina Melora Walters Michael Bowen

DESIGN FIRM Chogrin Inc.

LOCATION Guayaquil / Ecuador

SITE Chogrin.com

Night of the Creeps
10 × 16 in (25 × 41 cm)

クリープス 〜 スリル・ミー！

BEHIND THE POSTERS: I've been a *Ghostbusters* fan (aka "Ghosthead") since I was four. From the toys to the cereal, the GBs were a big part of my childhood and still are today. I chose to do this *Ghostbusters* piece [right] when I was invited to do the "Crazy for Cult 5" show at Gallery 1988 (Los Angeles). I wanted to portray the ultimate tribute that I could muster at that moment.

As for *Night of the Creeps*, I had grown up with *The Monster Squad*, and in my college years rediscovered it, along with other works from writer/film director Fred Dekker. In 2011, when I moved to L.A., I came across a flyer for a double-feature screening of *Night of the Creeps* and *The Monster Squad*, featuring a Q&A

with Fred. So, I approached Fred about making an appearance for an art show dedicated to both of his original films. Fred was thrilled to do it, and I created this poster in tribute to *Night of the Creeps* and for the event that was called "Monster Creeps" (Monstercreeps.blogspot.com).

INFLUENCES: I'd like to say my artwork is an amalgam of Popeye (E.C. Segar/The Fleischer Bros.), Astro Boy (Osamu Tezuka), and Willie Whopper (Ub Iwerks). But as with any artist, my artwork and what I create is a work in progress, and will always be influenced by new things and my changing surroundings.

And so I have various lists/categories of people that inspire me...

DESIGN FIRM	Chogrin Inc.
LOCATION	Guayaquil / Ecuador
SITE	Chogrin.com

In fine arts: Oswaldo Guayasamin, Diego Rivera, Frida Kahlo, Picasso, Henri Rousseau. In comics/manga: Osamu Tezuka, Marjane Satrapi, Mitsuteru Yokoyama, Shotaro Ishinomori, Mike Mignola, Brian Ralph, Aaron Renier, Brian Biggs, Akira Toriyama. In film: Steven Spielberg, Guillermo Del Toro, Fred Dekker, Alfonso Cuaron, Sebastian Cordero, Julie Taymor, Leslie Iwerks. In animation: Jorge Gutierrez, The Fleischer Bros, Aaron Augenblick, Shinchiro Watanabe, Yasuhiro Imagawa, Hayao Miyazaki. In music: Cafe Tacuba, Queen, Band of Horses, America, The Beatles, Mxpx, Screeching Weasel, Metallica, Nirvana, Yoko Kanno & The Seatbelts, and lots of film/tv/animation soundtracks.

FAVORITE FILM / GENRE: Adventure, sci-fi, and horror.
FIRST FILM: *Caveman* with Ringo Starr and Dennis Quaid.
PREFERRED MEDIUM: Blue and red lead mechanical pencils on 8 x 10" Strathmore sketchpad, vector (Adobe Illustrator), and watercolor.

They Live
24 x 36 in (61 x 91 cm)

Continued from page 7

BEHIND THE POSTERS: Regarding *They Live*: big fan of John Carpenter here. What can I say? I grew up in that era. His films just spoke to me. I was very fortunate to have a very cool mom who loved film as well. She would take me to see a lot of films that I shouldn't have seen. She would always talk with me afterwards about what we saw, and the difference between the movies and reality. I miss her!

The main influence for *They Live* was flyer poles/walls, where flyers for gigs or advertisements are pasted, and you get many different layers, colors, and textures. What's great about this film is that the message is so true. It still holds up. The scene in the bank is a classic. "I have come here to chew bubblegum and kick ass... and I'm all out of bubblegum." What a great line!

LOCATION Phoenix, Arizona / US

SITE Giantsumo.com

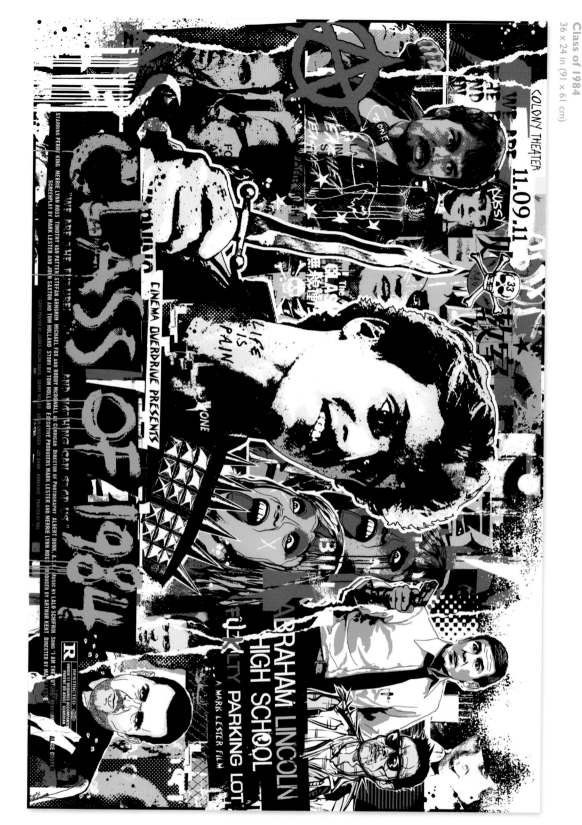

Class of 1984
36 × 24 in (91 × 61 cm)

Class of 1984 was a collaboration with Adam Martin, Jay Shaw, Danny Miller, and Boneface. I handled layout and art, and the guys were very cool to submit character art for me to work in to the poster. As with *They Live*, here I was influenced by the street flyer vibe and propaganda posters.

My mom brought *Class of 1984* home for me to watch when I was sick. I was in junior high and was like, "where the fuck does this happen?" I watched it three times in a row that night. Patsy made me feel funny in my pants. I also had that Stegman haircut. If I could go back in time, I would have kicked my own ass.

LOCATION Milton, Delaware / US

SITE Trevordunt.virb.com

Alien
11 x 17 in (28 x 43 cm)

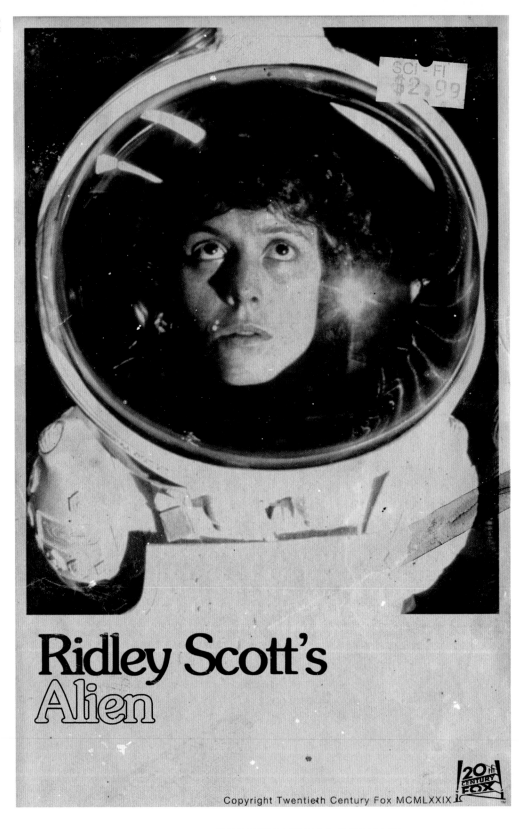

Ridley Scott's
Alien

Copyright Twentieth Century Fox MCMLXXIX

INFLUENCES: Saul Bass, Olly Moss, Midnight Marauder, Wes Anderson, and any odds and ends that I find through personal research of vintage graphic design.

FAVORITE FILM / GENRE: Horror.
PREFERRED MEDIUM: Digital.

Trevor Dunt

LOCATION	Milton, Delaware / US
SITE	Trevordunt.virb.com

WarGames
24 × 36 in (61 × 91 cm)

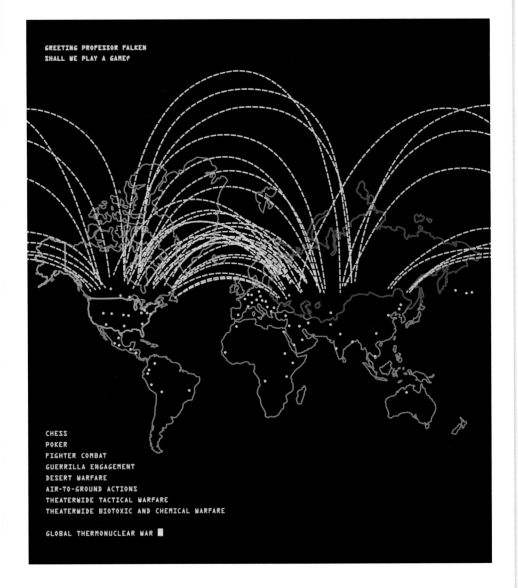

GREETING PROFESSOR FALKEN
SHALL WE PLAY A GAME?

CHESS
POKER
FIGHTER COMBAT
GUERRILLA ENGAGEMENT
DESERT WARFARE
AIR-TO-GROUND ACTIONS
THEATERWIDE TACTICAL WARFARE
THEATERWIDE BIOTOXIC AND CHEMICAL WARFARE

GLOBAL THERMONUCLEAR WAR ■

DIRECTED BY JOHN BADHAM

MATTHEW BRODERICK | ALLY SHEEDY | DABNEY COLEMAN | JOHN WOOD | BARRY CORBIN | MICHAEL MADSEN | WILLIAM H. MACY
SCREENPLAY BY LAWRENCE LASKER | WALTER F. PARKES | WALON GREEN | MUSIC BY ARTHUR B. RUBINSTEIN
CINEMATOGRAPHY BY WILLIAM A. FRAKER | EDITED BY TOM ROLF | 1983 | 114 MINUTES

Design: Matt Dupuis

ALIAS thegoodpope

LOCATION Guelph, Ontario / Canada

SITE Mattdupuis.com

BEHIND THE POSTERS: I don't buy new releases and instead choose to root through discount bins for what I consider "neglected cinematic gems." While I wouldn't say I am a big fan of these two specifically, I enjoyed them and was inspired to create these posters for different reasons.

I consider *Logan's Run* [right] to be a sci-fi classic. In 1976, it won an Academy Award for visual effects; the next year that same award went to *Star Wars,* and really that's all I think about while I'm watching it. *Star Wars* must have blown people's minds! *Logan's Run* has a great premise and cool scenes but mostly it just makes me laugh because the effects feel so dated.

With *WarGames* I was drawn to two things: the look of the WOPR supercomputer and the Atari Missile Command-style monitoring system of NORAD headquarters. The look of the technology reminded me of the golden age of video games.

INFLUENCES: For filmmakers, I'm influenced by anyone from Alejandro Jodorowsky to Wes Anderson. When it comes to design, I love Peter Saville's work with Factory Records, as well as posters by Saul Bass, Tom Jung, John Solie, and Bob Peak. I also love the layout of posters from the '60s, '70s and '80s (a favorite is *The Miracle Worker,* 1962).

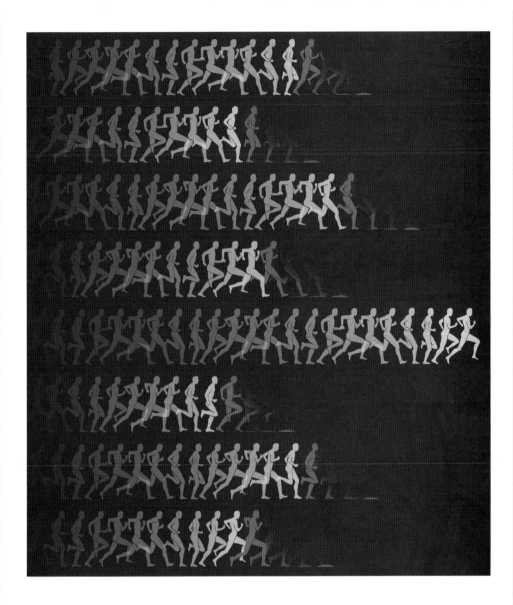

Logan's Run
24 x 36 in (61 x 91 cm)

Matt Dupuis

ALIAS thegoodpope
LOCATION Guelph, Ontario / Canada
SITE Mattdupuis.com

LOGAN'S RUN

DIRECTED BY MICHAEL ANDERSON

STARRING MICHAEL YORK | JENNY AGUTTER | RICHARD JORDAN | ROSCOE LEE BROWNE | FARRAH FAWCETT | PETER USTINOV
SCREENPLAY BY DAVID ZELAG GOODMAN | BASED ON THE NOVEL BY WILLIAM F. NOLAN | GEORGE CLAYTON JOHNSON
MUSIC BY JERRY GOLDSMITH | CINEMATOGRAPHY BY ERNEST LASZLO | EDITED BY BOB WYMAN | 1976 | 119 MINUTES

Design: Matt Dupuis

FAVORITE FILM / GENRE: *Bottle Rocket* is probably my favorite film. It was simple, funny, heartwarming, and stylish. I showed the film to my friends and half of them didn't laugh once. The other half went out and bought jumpsuits with me.

FIRST FILM: My parents say that the first time they heard me laugh at the TV was when Dorothy slapped the Cowardly Lion in *The Wizard of Oz*. I also remember watching *Star Wars* on video disc (and having to get someone to flip the disc halfway through the movie). But the first movie that I remember seeing in the theatre was *The Last Starfighter*. I was four, and my mom and aunt made me hide under my coat during the "scary" parts.

PREFERRED MEDIUM: I like the challenge of creating an image out of vectors and having it be scalable. But when I get an idea, I like to stage photos or collages, like my posters for *Videodrome, Close Encounters of the Third Kind,* and *The Birds* (which involved scanning real feathers).

Queen of Outer Space
18 x 24 in (46 x 61 cm)

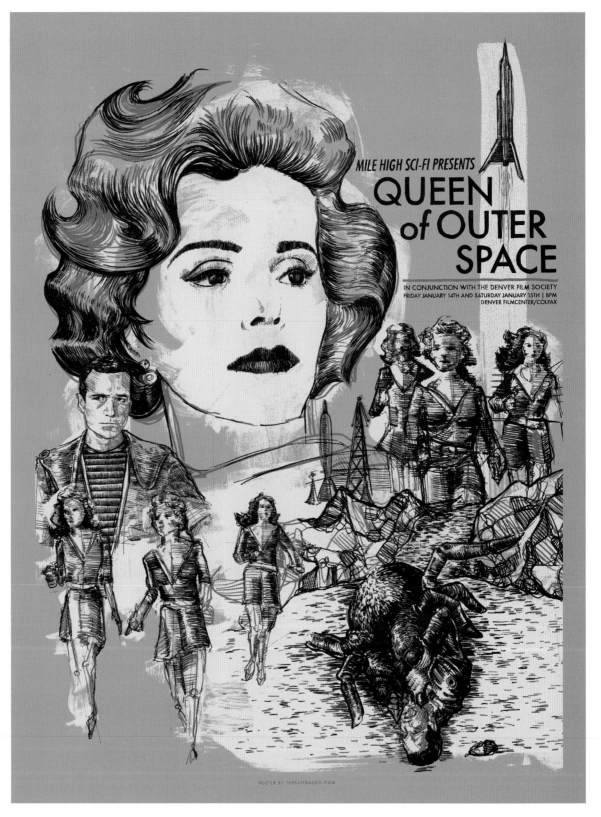

DESIGN FIRM The Bungaloo!
LOCATION Denver, Colorado / US
SITE Thebungaloo.com

BEHIND THE POSTERS: Both of these were done for a comedy group in town, Mile High Sci-Fi. They spoof and comment on movies as they're playing in the theatre.

INFLUENCES: Bill Watterson, Gary Larson, McBess.
FIRST FILM: *Dumbo.*
PREFERRED MEDIUM: Pen and ink, screen print.

▶ John Vogl

DESIGN FIRM The Bungaloo!
LOCATION Denver, Colorado / US
SITE Thebungaloo.com

LOCATION Lille / France

SITE Guillaumevasseur.fr + Thisisdwid.tumblr.com

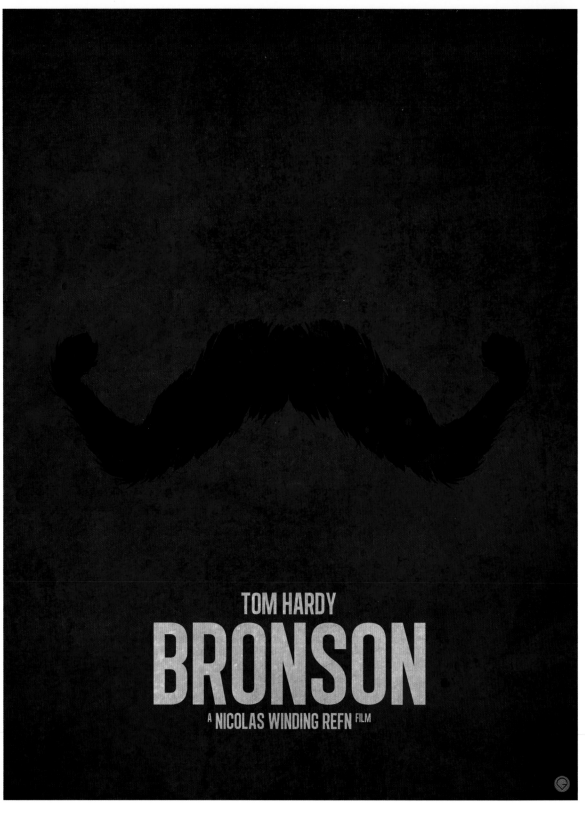

TOM HARDY
BRONSON
A NICOLAS WINDING REFN FILM

BEHIND THE POSTER: This poster is actually the first one that I ever made. After watching Nicolas Winding Refn's *Bronson*, which was a visually brilliant movie, I was obsessed with the image of a blood-soaked, glorious moustache. At that time I was seeing a lot of very clever fan-made movie posters, and wanted to give it a shot.

INFLUENCES: Painters/designers/digital artists such as Mark Rothko, Olly Moss, Gerhard Richter, Francis Bacon, Mike Mignola, Saul Bass, Frank Miller, Karl Kwasny, Mike Mitchell, Rob Sheridan, and more.

Film directors: Stanley Kubrick, Nicolas Winding Refn, David Fincher, Quentin Tarantino, Akira Kurosawa, Takeshi Kitano, Darren Aronofsky, David Cronenberg, etc.

FAVORITE FILM / GENRE: Probably Kubrick's *2001: A Space Odyssey*.

FIRST FILM: I think one of my first mind-blowing experiences was watching *The Exorcist* at age seven, and Kubrick's *A Clockwork Orange* and *2001: A Space Odyssey* a few years later.

PREFERRED MEDIUM: Digital is the best way to create what I really have in mind. But it's also nice to work with good old pencil/ink and paper from time to time.

LOCATION Berlin / Germany

SITE Malatesta.mysupadupa.com

BEHIND THE POSTER: *Machete* is absurd, violent, and funny at the same time...and absolutely insane. Good stuff.

INFLUENCES: I really like the art of Georg Baselitz, with its upside-down motifs and the vibrancy of the colors. Among the artists who I have followed lately, I'd say Neck Face and Cleon Peterson. But one of the designers that I most appreciate is definitely Saul Bass. He was ridiculously talented.

FAVORITE FILM / GENRE: It depends on the moment and my mood. The problem for me is staying awake. I'm terrible. I'll sleep in the cinema during a scene of a nuclear bombing. It happened.

FIRST FILM: *One Flew Over the Cuckoo's Nest*.

PREFERRED MEDIUM: I always begin with a ballpoint pen and a sheet of paper. Then I digitize the whole thing.

ADDITIONAL REMARKS: Learn something every day.

More artwork from Rocco Malatesta on page 161

Fight Club
28 x 38 in (70 x 97 cm)

LOCATION Melbourne, Victoria / Australia
SITE Deechoi.com + Society6.com/deechoi

BEHIND THE POSTER: I saw another fan poster for it online, which made me want to watch the movie, which made me want to make a fan poster for it.
INFLUENCES: Saul Bass, Olly Moss, Quentin Tarantino, Banksy, Leonardo Da Vinci.
FAVORITE FILM / GENRE: *The Matrix, Inglourious Basterds, Spirited Away, Oldboy, 8 Mile, Aladdin, American Psycho, The Prestige, Battle Royale, My Sassy Girl, Zoolander.*

FIRST FILM: *Aladdin.*
PREFERRED MEDIUM: Brush and paint, or Illustrator and Photoshop.
ADDITIONAL REMARKS: I am employable for all your design needs. Past experiences: full-time madcunt, part-time sickcunt.

DESIGN FIRM dannDESIGNS
LOCATION Superior, Wisconsin / US
SITE Danndesigns.com

BEHIND THE POSTER: I started a project re-imagining posters of my favorite movies. This was the black sheep of the collection. *Black Dynamite* had too many memorable scenes, so I simplified the title into an icon that was as tongue-in-cheek as the movie itself.

INFLUENCES: Saul Bass and Olly Moss sparked my interested in starting this project.

FAVORITE FILM / GENRE: Depressing drama. I watch a lot of comedy, but movies, like *City of God,* that leave me emotionally distressed really have an impact on me.

FIRST FILM: *Star Wars Episode VI: Return of the Jedi,* when I was two. I hope that I was quiet.

PREFERRED MEDIUM: I've been working solely in Illustrator and Photoshop for years now. I would like to get back into oil painting someday.

ADDITIONAL REMARKS: I tried my hand at a Saul Bass-inspired recreation of the *Clerks* movie intro. I think that movie intros are the natural extension of poster recreations.

Mile 44

The Godfather
18 x 24 in (46 x 61 cm)

DESIGNERS Dave Windisch and Stacy Curtis

LOCATION Chicago, Illinois and Indianapolis, Indiana / US

SITE Mile44.com

Continued from page 27

BEHIND THE POSTER: [Dave]: *The Godfather*. So many memorable scenes here. The restaurant assassination, "Leave the gun. Take the cannoli," the closing door at the end. *The Godfather* entrenches the viewer, making them feel like they've actually become a family member. My mom and I always refer to the moment when Sonny is gunned down at the toll booth as one of our favorite, most emotional moments in film.

LOCATION | Paris / France

SITE | Maximepecourt.blogspot.fr + Society6.com/maximepecourt

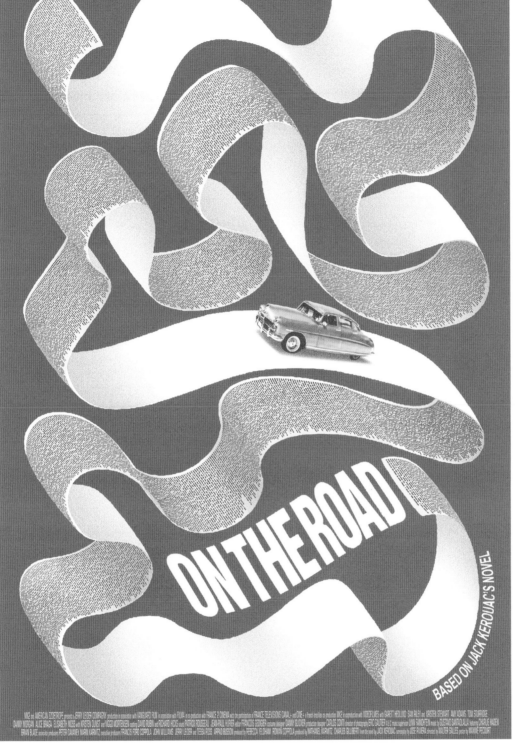

BEHIND THE POSTER: *ShortList* magazine asked me to design a poster for the wide release of the movie. But prior to creating the poster, I wanted to read the book, and then see the film (which was already released in France).

I wanted something here that was very graphic and minimalist at first sight, yet complex in the details, with colors from the 1950s.
FAVORITE FILM / GENRE: I love cinema in general but my favorite movies are *Casablanca, Jules et Jim, The Empire Strikes Back, Singin' in the Rain, Beauty and the Beast* by Cocteau, *Aladdin* by Disney, etc.

FIRST FILM: The first film that I really remember seeing was *Dreams* by Kurosawa. Later, *Raiders of the Lost Ark* and *E.T.* on VHS.
PREFERRED MEDIUM: I often use computers, but also love to use my hands with pencils, paper cutting, etc.
ADDITIONAL REMARKS: I also direct clips and short films.

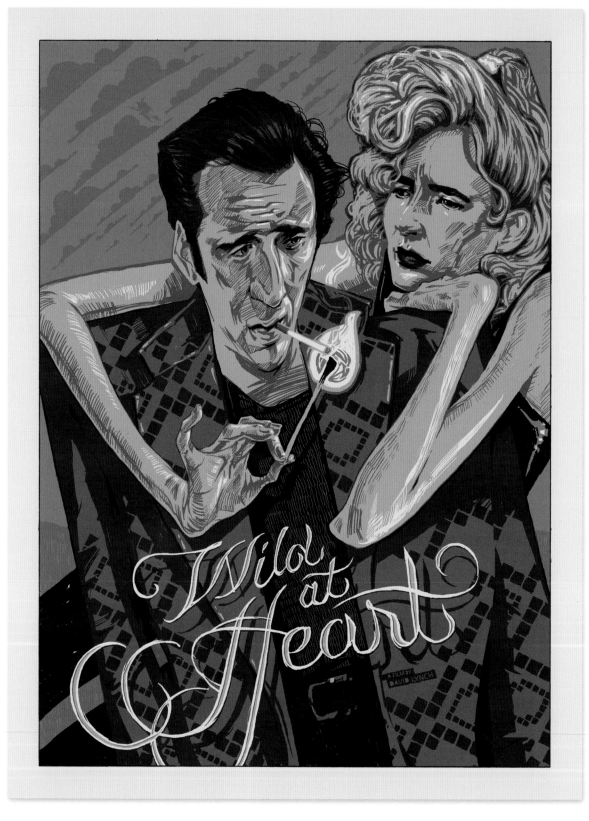

BEHIND THE POSTERS: Both of these images were contributions to gallery shows. *Wild at Heart* was part of an exhibition called "Oh, You Are Sick..." at Phone Booth Gallery, celebrating the films of David Lynch. The *King of Kong* print is titled *Kill Screen* and was part of a video game-inspired show at Gallery 1988 entitled "Multiplayer."

David Lynch is such a unique voice, a breath of fresh (but disturbing) air. Any time I need to get out of my comfort zone or look at something from a different point of view, I'll turn to David Lynch. Also, much like everyone else who saw *King of Kong*, I became obsessed overnight with the culture surrounding the quest for high scores in arcade games. The obsession culminated in this print [right].

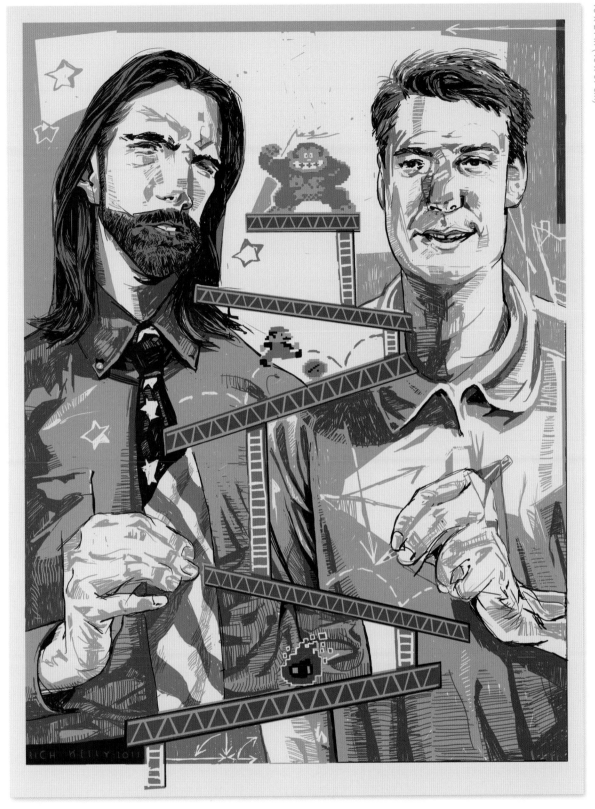

INFLUENCES: Lately I have been looking a lot at Terry Gilliam, Paul Thomas Anderson, and The Coen Brothers as an influence on both my design chops and storytelling ability.

FAVORITE FILM / GENRE: Time and time again I go back to *Confessions of a Dangerous Mind*. Charlie Kaufman is one of my favorite screenwriters and Sam Rockwell is hilarious and tragic at the same time. A clever story and creative execution make this one of my favorites for sure.

FIRST FILM: As a young child in suburban Pennsylvania, *The Goonies* pretty much instilled in me a sense of wonder and curiosity that remains with me to this day. I should probably grow up, but I still can't shake that desire to go on adventures, explore the unknown.

PREFERRED MEDIUM: Pencil on paper—the most reliable and steadfast tools for translating the communication between my eyes and hands.

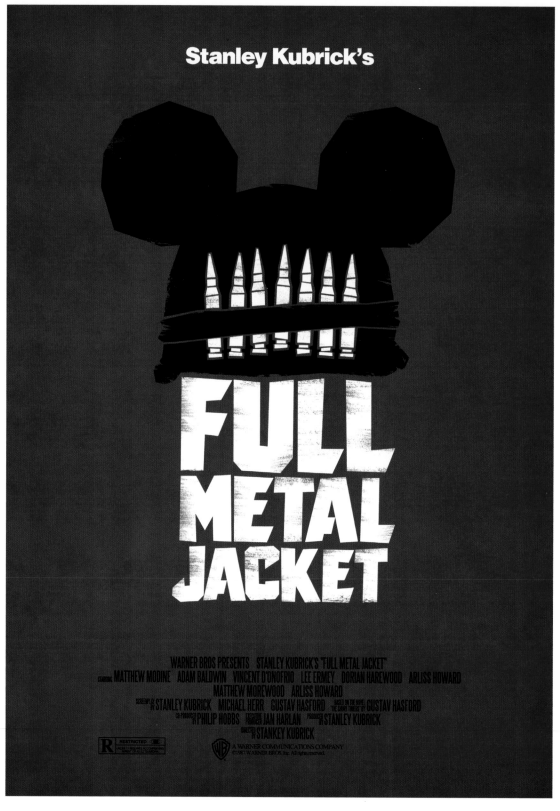

Stanley Kubrick's

FULL METAL JACKET

WARNER BROS PRESENTS · STANLEY KUBRICK'S "FULL METAL JACKET"
STARRING MATTHEW MODINE · ADAM BALDWIN · VINCENT D'ONOFRIO · LEE ERMEY · DORIAN HAREWOOD · ARLISS HOWARD
MATTHEW MOREWOOD · ARLISS HOWARD
SCREENPLAY BY STANLEY KUBRICK · MICHAEL HERR · GUSTAV HASFORD · BASED ON THE NOVEL "THE SHORT TIMERS" BY GUSTAV HASFORD
CO-PRODUCER PHILIP HOBBS · EXECUTIVE PRODUCER JAN HARLAN · PRODUCED BY STANLEY KUBRICK
DIRECTED BY STANLEY KUBRICK

A WARNER COMMUNICATIONS COMPANY
©1987 WARNER BROS. Inc. All rights reserved.

BEHIND THE POSTERS: The poster for *Full Metal Jacket* was requested by Cinematheque Francaise, which in 2011 organized an exhibition dedicated to the works of Stanley Kubrick. *Escape from New York* [right] was a personal piece—I'm a big fan.

In the poster for Kubrick's masterpiece, *Full Metal Jacket,* I used typical military colors, as well as a stencil style similar to what the military uses for lettering vehicles and infrastructure. Also, the film sequence where soldiers marched to the "Mickey Mouse March" is one of *Full Metal Jacket*'s most iconic moments, so I

represented it by inserting the famous mouse ears on a military helmet. The artwork depicts similar elements to the original theatrical poster, but with additional symbolism.

For *Escape from New York,* I tried to group multiple items into a single image. New York City is represented by the apple, with the snake protagonist running through it. In addition, the merging of two elements compose the outline of the eye patch worn by Kurt Russell.

INFLUENCES: Saul Bass, Sergio Leone, Quentin Tarantino, Italian posters, Mondotees.

FAVORITE FILM / GENRE: Thrillers, spaghetti westerns, horror, sci-fi, comedy. My favorite film is *The Good, the Bad, and the Ugly.*

PREFERRED MEDIUM: I use vector graphics, paper, and pencil.

ADDITIONAL REMARKS: After the release of *Kill Bill Vol. 1* in 2003, the works of Quentin Tarantino strongly inspired me on a creative level. In Spring 2011, a few days after the title of Tarantino's new film, *Django Unchained,* was announced, I created a poster. Many sites that didn't yet have access to official images used my artwork to discuss the film. In the summer of 2011, one of my *Django Unchained* one-sheets was posted on Quentin Tarantino's Facebook page, and a few days later I was contacted by his film production house; they wanted to use the image in the film's promotional campaign. This included clothing for the staff and crew passes. It was also used as the basis for the official teaser poster, which contains a similar style and the same colors as my poster.

Tarantino also asked if I could send him a series of posters devoted to Italian cinema. Since he is easily my favorite living director, this was an absolute dream.

The Goonies
11 x 11 in (28 x 28 cm)

LOCATION New Jersey / US

SITE Hasunow.com

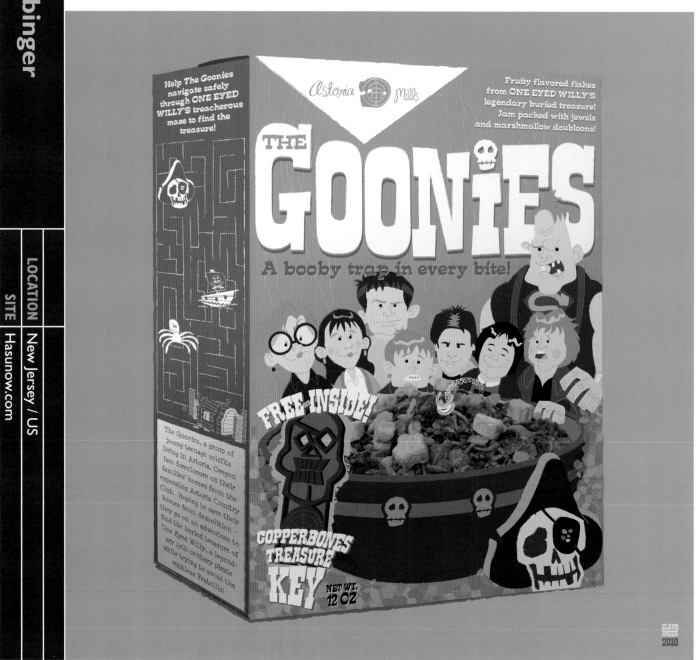

BEHIND THE POSTERS: These were created for "3G" back in 2010 as three individual giclée canvas prints. The show was a tribute to the classic '80s movies: *The Goonies, Ghostbusters,* and *Gremlins.* I called the series *Part of this Complete Breakfast.* The idea to make the films into cereal boxes came about when I was food shopping. I saw a cereal box that had an ad for an upcoming movie tie-in and thought to myself, "What would happen if the cereal was transformed into that movie, rather than just coming with a toy or movie ticket?" I also knew that some of these movies were likely made into actual cereals back in the '80s, but mine were meant to be more of a spoof.

Back to the Future [see Ian's site] was the fourth and final print added to this series, and was created as a custom commission; a purchaser loved the series so much that he wanted his favorite film [*Back to the Future*] recreated in the same style.
INFLUENCES: First and foremost is all things retro. I love the style of the 1940s through the 1960s—the animation, decor, advertising, architecture, fashion, etc. I also love the works of Walt Disney (and his lovely theme parks), Tex Avery, Chuck Jones, UPA

Gremlins
11 x 11 in (28 x 28 cm)

LOCATION New Jersey / US

SITE Hasunow.com

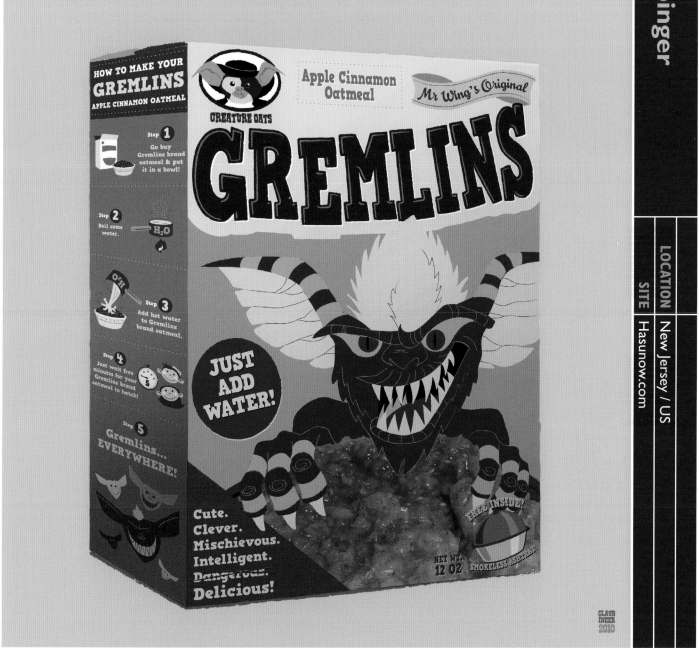

HOW TO MAKE YOUR
GREMLINS
APPLE CINNAMON OATMEAL

CREATURE OATS

Apple Cinnamon
Oatmeal

Mr Wing's Original

GREMLINS

Step 1
Go buy
Gremlins brand
oatmeal & put
it in a bowl!

Step 2
Boil some
water.

H₂O

Step 3
Add hot water
to Gremlins
brand oatmeal.

Step 4
Just wait five
minutes for your
Gremlins brand
oatmeal to hatch!

Step 5
Gremlins...
EVERYWHERE!

JUST
ADD
WATER!

FREE INSIDE!

Cute.
Clever.
Mischievous.
Intelligent.
Dangerous.
Delicious!

NET WT.
12 OZ   SMOKELESS ASHTRAY

GLAUB
INGER
2010

cartoons, and Hanna-Barbera. Currently, I'm really big into artists like Derek Yaniger, Christopher Lee (not the *Lord of the Rings* guy), Matt Kaufenberg, Kevin Dart, Dave Perillo, Joey Ellis, Andrew Kolb, and more. And last but not least, my lovely wife, Kim! Also, my cat Dex would be pretty mad if I didn't acknowledge him.
FAVORITE FILM / GENRE: I love all genres, except maybe musicals. But hands down, my favorite movie of all time is *Who Framed Roger Rabbit?*

FIRST FILM: *Beetlejuice* (1988). I was six at the time and it scared me half to death. My dad and sister stayed for the entire movie while my mom took me out of the theater, where I distinctly remember sitting in the carpeted hallway playing with those little plastic one-color dinosaurs. I also had a nightmare that same evening. I ruled.
PREFERRED MEDIUM: It all starts with pencil and paper for me. However, I also use Illustrator and a Wacom Cintiq (fancy drawing tablet) with Photoshop to make things pretty and colorful.

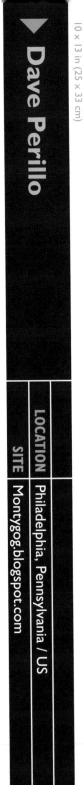

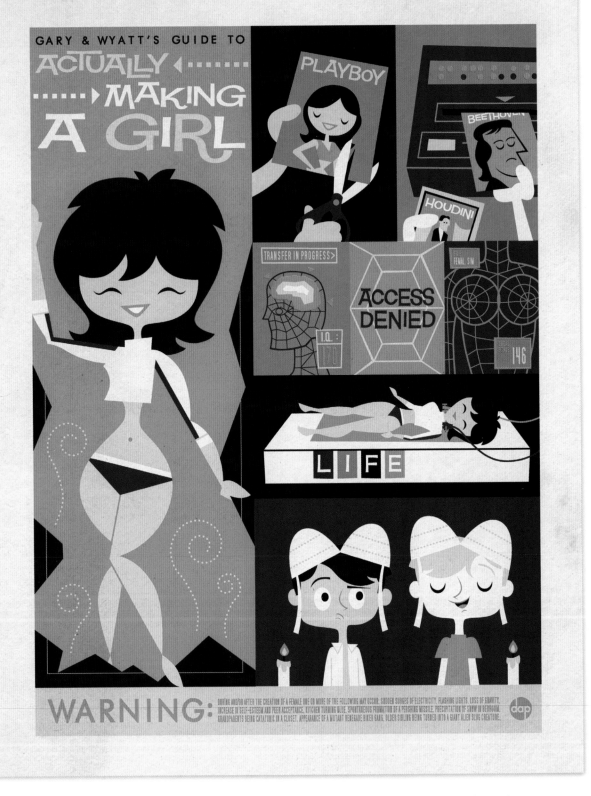

BEHIND THE POSTERS: I'm a huge fan of both *Weird Science* and *Better Off Dead*, which lead to these posters.
INFLUENCES: Charles Schulz, Jim Henson, Rod Serling, Alfred Hitchcock, Jim Flora, Mary Blair, Roy Lichtenstein.

FAVORITE FILM / GENRE: It's tough to choose just one film or genre, but I'd say that my favorite decade for movies is the 1980s. The 1980s had some of my all-time favorites, but was also the last time when single or twin-house movie theaters reigned before all of the multiplexes started popping up. There was such a charm to sitting in a one-house or two-house theater that would keep a movie for weeks before it would get something new. This was also the dawn of VHS rental stores, and seeing films that I had never heard of before. I still remember the first movie that my family rented for our first VCR: *The Toy,* starring Richard Pryor and Jackie Gleason.

Better Off Dead (actual title = Go that Way Really Fast...)
18 × 12 in (46 × 30 cm)

FIRST FILM: The first movie that I remember seeing in a theater was Disney's *The Cat from Outer Space*. I was a little under four years old.

PREFERRED MEDIUM: Adobe Illustrator to create the work, and screen printing to produce the finished piece.

ADDITIONAL REMARKS: I think that it's fantastic that artists are making alternative movie posters. It harkens back to when Hollywood would create an exciting piece of art for its posters, as opposed to one slapped together in Photoshop.

ALIAS / DESIGN FIRM
QFSChris of Quiltface Studios

LOCATION
Philadelphia, Pennsylvania / US

SITE
Quiltfacestudios.tumblr.com
+ Quiltfacestudios.storenvy.com

BEHIND THE POSTERS: I've been a regular poster designer for The Colonial Theatre [Phoenixville, Pennsylvania], which is local to me and famous for being the theatre where the original classic, *The Blob,* was filmed. They host what's been dubbed "First Friday Fright Nights," which are 35mm screenings of classic and current horror films. *Popcorn* [right] was a very rare screening opportunity, and being a major fan of this underrated gem, I jumped at the chance to do the poster. *Black Christmas* was the print that marked my one year anniversary with The Colonial, so aside from being a huge fan, I also have a sentimental attachment to the poster design.

INFLUENCES: Oh man, so many! N.E. over at New Flesh Prints, John Lucero of Black Label Skateboards, Jay Shaw, Ghoulish Gary Pullin, Charles Moran (aka "Zomic"), and everyone in the "Print Posse" are tops as far as designers go. Also, I'm pretty much constantly influenced by the artistic blend of beauty and brutality that Quentin Tarantino delivers.

ALIAS / DESIGN FIRM QFSChris of Quiltface Studios

LOCATION Philadelphia, Pennsylvania / US

SITE Quiltfacestudios.tumblr.com
+ Quiltfacestudios.storenvy.com

FAVORITE FILM / GENRE: Horror/exploitation, hands-down.
FIRST FILM: The original, 1974 *Texas Chainsaw Massacre*...that film struck a nerve to the core, and I've been a horror nut ever since.
PREFERRED MEDIUM: Screen printing. Nothing beats ink on paper.

ADDITIONAL REMARKS: Fellow creatives: appreciate and reciprocate. We're all cut from the same cloth, we just wear it differently. Keep it fun.

BEHIND THE POSTER: I went through my list of favorite movies, looking for something I could play around with in poster form. I thought about *Clue* and came up with a neat way to get the point of the movie across. That's what it all comes down to: something clever that says a lot with very little.

INFLUENCES: Saul Bass. There's no one that compares to Saul Bass' posters. They were the essence of style. Brandon Schaefer also does some amazing minimalist movie posters, and it was his work that inspired me to give it a try.

FAVORITE FILM / GENRE: *The Usual Suspects*. That's the movie that I wish that I had written. Any story with that kind of duplicity and manipulation is something that I'll always be drawn to. Liars, cheaters, thieves: nothing better.

FIRST FILM: That I ever saw? *Gorillas in the Mist*, apparently, though I have no memory of it.

PREFERRED MEDIUM: Adobe Illustrator. That's all I've got the know-how for.

Alien
10 x 14 in (25 x 36 cm)

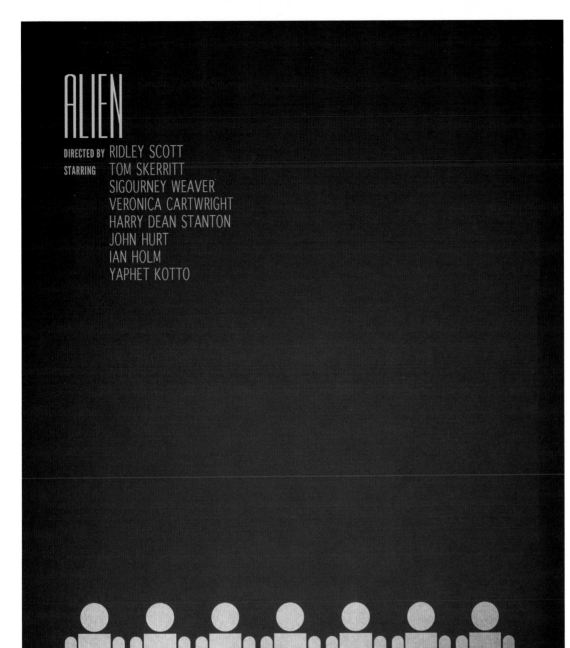

ALIEN
DIRECTED BY RIDLEY SCOTT
STARRING TOM SKERRITT
SIGOURNEY WEAVER
VERONICA CARTWRIGHT
HARRY DEAN STANTON
JOHN HURT
IAN HOLM
YAPHET KOTTO

LOCATION Lille / France

SITE Sammarkiewi.cz

BEHIND THE POSTER: I was watching an *Alien* marathon and noticed that each director applied his own style and mark to the films: Ridley Scott created the story line, James Cameron transformed it into an action movie, Fincher gave it a spiritual and more philosophical feel, and Jean-Pierre Jeunet made a piece of s***. I translated these ideas into images and came up with four posters, one of which you see here.

INFLUENCES: Pet Shop Boys, James A. Reeves, Chuck Palahniuk, Mark Farrow, John Carpenter, several post-hardcore bands, Steven Spielberg, my art school director, Jean-Claude Schenkel, my lady friend, and a long list of people, anonymous or not, that inspire me every day.

FAVORITE FILM / GENRE: The Korean wave of thriller movies. They are beautiful, uncompromising, poetic, and meaningful films. If you haven't seen any, start with *The Yellow Sea* and *The Chaser*!

FIRST FILM: It was *Oliver & Company*, with my dear and beloved mom, who took her afternoon off to spend some time with her son.

ADDITIONAL REMARKS: "You can be childlike without being childish. A child always wants to have fun. Ask yourself, 'Am I having fun?'" –Christopher Meloni

Bambi
12 x 17 in (30 x 43 cm)

DESIGN FIRM Rowan Stocks-Moore Design

LOCATION London / UK

SITE Rowanstocksmoore.com + Etsy.com/shop/rowansm

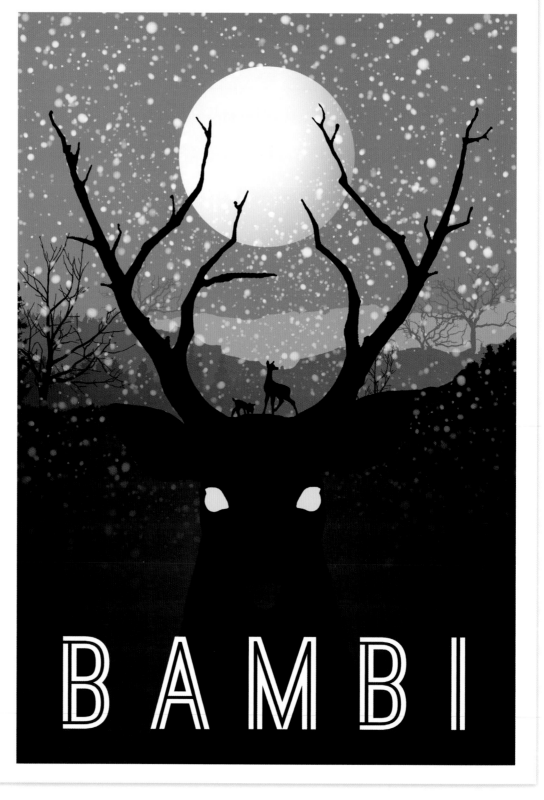

BEHIND THE POSTERS: I'm a fan of Disney in general and have been since I was a child. Both of these films are tinged with darker aspects that I love, but also steeped in the lightheartedness that has made Disney so popular with fans of all ages.

INFLUENCES: My chief influences are Saul Bass and Tim Burton. Bass' simple, bold designs have been a major inspiration, and Burton's gothic stylings have fed my imagination and added to my love of all things dark and twisted!

Peter Pan
12 x 17 in (30 x 43 cm)

DESIGN FIRM	Rowan Stocks-Moore Design
LOCATION	London / UK
SITE	Rowanstocksmoore.com + Etsy.com/shop/rowansm

FAVORITE FILM / GENRE: I struggle to choose favorites, but as you can imagine, I love *Edward Scissorhands*. It was the first Burton film that I saw and remains my favorite of his movies, with *Beetlejuice* coming a close second. Both are darkly comic and filled with visual jokes that have served as an inspiration for my film poster designs.

FIRST FILM: One of the first was certainly *FernGully: The Last Rainforest*.

PREFERRED MEDIUM: I don't have one preferred medium; instead I like to combine traditional pencil or pen illustrations with work on Photoshop and Illustrator to achieve a hand-drawn, yet clean and consistent appearance.

UP
11 x 17 in (28 x 43 cm)

UP

A Film By Disney • Pixar

BEHIND THE POSTER: I love all of Pixar's films. Carl's story in *Up* is very touching and provided great inspiration for the print (e.g., "Where there is a will, there is a way"…"We need to keep our promises"…etc.).

INFLUENCES: To name a few: Hayao Miyazaki, Ang Lee, Steven Spielberg, Jerry Bruckheimer, Christopher Nolan, Tim Burton.

FAVORITE FILM / GENRE: Animation, action, adventure, fantasy.

FIRST FILM: *Toy Story,* my all-time favorite!

PREFERRED MEDIUM: I prefer both traditional and digital methods.

Christian Jackson

ALIAS	Square Inch Design
LOCATION	Chicago, Illinois / US
SITE	Squareinchdesign.com

THE WIZARD OF OZ

L. FRANK BAUM | SERIES 04

BEHIND THE POSTER: It's part of a greater "Classic Children's Story" series that I completed in 2010.
INFLUENCES: Paul Rand and Tim Boelaars.

FAVORITE FILM / GENRE: *Perfume: The Story of a Murderer.*
PREFERRED MEDIUM: I'm a digital guy.

Dani Blázquez

Terminator 2: Judgment Day
28 x 39 in (70 x 100 cm)

LOCATION Salamanca / Spain
SITE Behance.net/daniblazquez

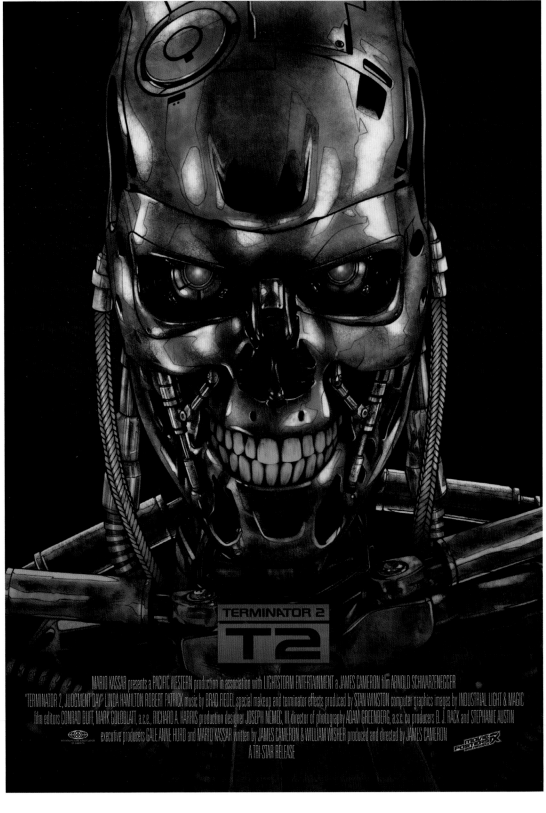

BEHIND THE POSTERS: These two posters are part of my *FX Movie Posters* series. I wanted to pay tribute to some of the titles that marked special effects milestones in the history of cinema.
INFLUENCES: I particularly loved the aesthetics of the '80s–'90s. However, focusing on movie poster design, I love the techniques of Nick Runge, Mike Butkus, and, of course, Drew Struzan. I also love the posters of John Alvin, Richard Amsel, Frank Frazetta, Bob Peak, Birney Lettick, Tom Jung, Renato Casaro.... In short, movie poster designers from the 1950s to the mid-1990s. My favorite current designers include GABZ, Martin Ansin, Tyler Stout, Olly Moss, and Daniel Danger.

FAVORITE FILM / GENRE: What a difficult question! I do love movies from the '80s and early '90s, not so much for the film quality (some are really bad), but for the nostalgia and the aesthetics. I've seen some films from this era hundreds of times.

Dani Blázquez

LOCATION Salamanca / Spain

SITE Behance.net/daniblazquez

TRON

Disney's

A LISBERGER- KUSHNER PRODUCTION
STARRING JEFF BRIDGES
BRUCE BOXLEITNER DAVID WARNER
CINDY MORGAN AND BARNARD HUGHES
EXECUTIVE PRODUCER RON MILLER MUSIC BY WENDY CARLOS
STORY BY STEVEN LISBERGER AND BONNIE MACBIRD
SCREENPLAY BY STEVEN LISBERGER PRODUCED BY DONALD KUSHNER
SONGS BY JOURNEY FROM WALT DISNEY PRODUCTIONS
DIRECTED BY STEVEN LIBERGER

FIRST FILM: I can't quite remember my very first film, but I do remember scenes from early movies. For example, the transformation of Nastassja Kinski (with Bowie in the background) in *Cat People*. Or the scene with the tobacconist in *Amarcord* ("… no, I can breathe…!"). I remember being glued to my chair for these two scenes.

PREFERRED MEDIUM: I like to draw and subsequently retouch with digital color.

MST3K SUPER FRIENDS CLUB PROUDLY PRESENTS

SANTA CLAUS

AS PART OF THE MST3K DRINK & DRAW SERIES

WEDNESDAY, AUGUST 4TH, 2010 9 PM EST

WATCH ALONG ON NETFLIX. DRAW ALONG WITH THE MOVIE.
FOLLOW ALONG ON TWITTER WITH @THECHRISHALEY AND
@THEJENYA OR FIND ALL THE GREAT TWEETS USING THE
HASHTAG #MST3KDANDD.

BEHIND THE POSTERS: Both were electronically distributed posters for a weekly Twitter-based "Drink & Draw" event, where anybody who was interested could watch the film and draw along, posting their drawings and observations on Twitter as they went. The event was run by the incredibly talented cartoonists Chris Haley and Jen Vaughn. For both of the films here, I went in relatively blind, having only seen bits of *Santa Claus* on *Mystery Science Theater 3000*.

INFLUENCES: My favorite designers include Bradbury Thompson, Jim Flora, Stefan Sagmeister, Milton Glaser, Art Chantry, Tadanori Yokoo, Michael Beirut, Chip Kidd, Alvin Lustig, and Paul Sahre. My favorite film directors: Woody Allen, The Coen Brothers, Alfred Hitchcock, Robert Altman, Federico Fellini, Wes Anderson, Stanley Kubrick, Spike Jonze, Francis Ford Coppola, Steven Spielberg, Michel Gondry, and Jim Jarmusch.

My favorite food is pizza.

▼ **Dylan Todd**

LOCATION Las Vegas, Nevada / US

SITE Bigredrobot.net + Dylantodd.com

THE MST3K SUPER FRIENDS CLUB PROUDLY PRESENTS

BATMAN
VERSUS
DRACULA

AS PART OF THE MYSTERY SCIENCE THEATER 3000 DRINK & DRAW SERIES.

WEDNESDAY, OCTOBER 27, 2010 MOVIESIGN AT 9 PM, EST

Watch along on Netflix. Draw along with the movie. Follow along on Twitter with @thechrishaley
and @thejenya or find all the great tweets using the hashtag #MST3KDANDD.

FAVORITE FILM / GENRE: Is there a genre of movie where Draculas on dirt bikes fight robots who shoot lasers from their eyes?
FIRST FILM: It was either *Star Wars* or *Sgt. Pepper's Lonely Hearts Club Band;* you know, that really terrible one where the Bee Gees and Peter Frampton sing '70s-ified versions of Beatles songs? Both films were formative for me. This explains a lot.

PREFERRED MEDIUM: I primarily work digitally, but I'll jump at any chance I have to get my hands dirty.
ADDITIONAL REMARKS: I've also created some packaging redesigns for movies that will most likely never be inducted into the prestigious Fake Criterions website, including one for the Nicolas Cage version of *The Wicker Man*. It was for a contest. I won a pair of Nicolas Cage's pants.

DESIGN FIRM	Slasher Design
LOCATION	Lawrence, Kansas / US
SITE	Osbourndraw.com + Slasherdesign.blogspot.com

BEHIND THE POSTER: *Silent Night, Deadly Night* was created for Fright Rags, a horror clothing company. Subsequently it was made into a t-shirt as well.

INFLUENCES: To name just a few: Bob Ross, Ed Repka, Jason Edmiston, and Tom "The Dude" Hodge.

FAVORITE FILM / GENRE: Slasher and exploitation films of the '70s and '80s. The overall aesthetic, look, and mood of that era really catches my eye. A little cheese thrown in is usually a good thing, too.

FIRST FILM: Nothing has affected me like *Night of the Living Dead* did when I first saw it. It was back when they still showed midnight monster flicks on Saturday night. It scared the hell out me and gave me nightmares. I've probably seen it close to a thousand times over the years. It's absolutely beautiful, and looks and feels so real.

PREFERRED MEDIUM: I grew up drawing and painting with acrylics, but today I prefer digital. It's a lot easier to make edits or alterations if you have a happy little accident.

More artwork from Justin Osbourn on pages 198 and 199

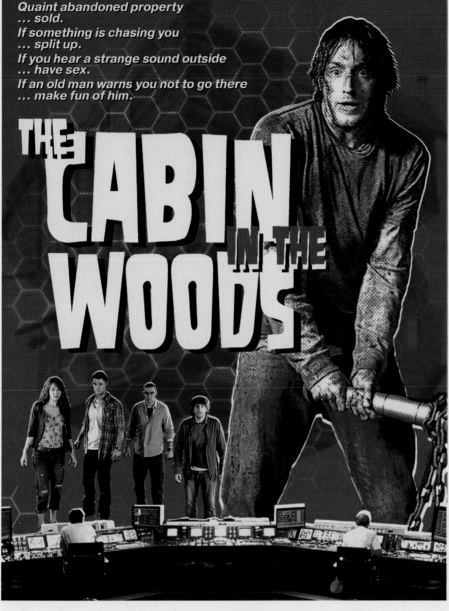

BEHIND THE POSTER: Since I create film posters for fun, I only choose films that I love, and *The Cabin in the Woods* is a fantastic parody of slasher films.

INFLUENCES: Alfred Hitchcock, Tim Burton, Saul Bass, Dave McKean, my husband, mother, and father.

FAVORITE FILM / GENRE: I love dark fairy tales, horror, and adventure.

FIRST FILM: I remember watching a lot of Russian fairy tales as a child, but one of the first movies that I remember very clearly was *Back to the Future*. I was six.

PREFERRED MEDIUM: Camera, Photoshop, and imagination.

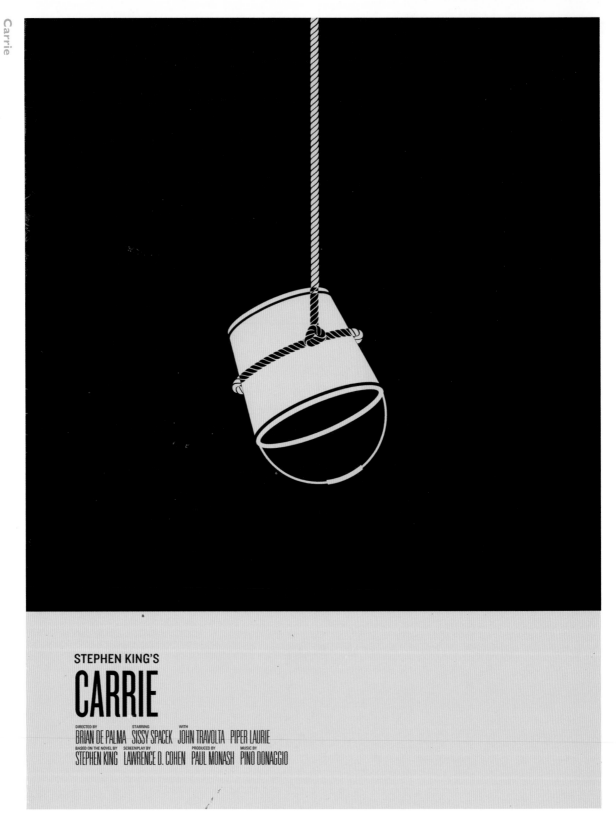

BEHIND THE POSTERS: I was looking for a series of films to distill into a simple one-color poster. I'm a big Stephen King fan so his movies seemed like the perfect fit. Each of his films seems to have additional layers of "scary" underneath, and I wanted to convey this in a very simple way.

INFLUENCES: I am always influenced by movies that have hidden messages and inside jokes. I've always appreciated subtlety in movies and for this series I challenged myself on translating that idea into poster form.

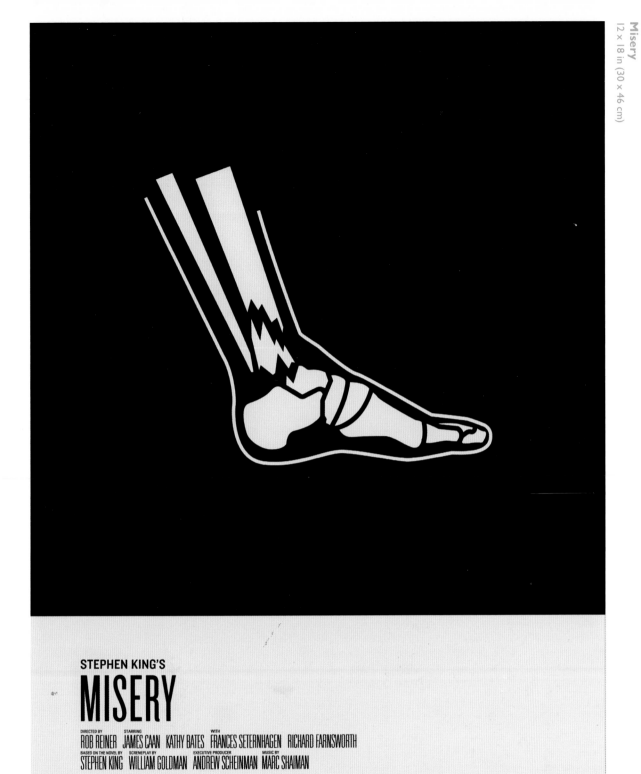

STEPHEN KING'S
MISERY

DIRECTED BY ROB REINER STARRING JAMES CAAN KATHY BATES WITH FRANCES SETERNHAGEN RICHARD FARNSWORTH
BASED ON THE NOVEL BY STEPHEN KING SCREENPLAY BY WILLIAM GOLDMAN EXECUTIVE PRODUCER ANDREW SCHEINMAN MUSIC BY MARC SHAIMAN

FAVORITE FILM / GENRE: I love Hitchcock and slow-burning film noirs.

FIRST FILM: *Fantasia*.
PREFERRED MEDIUM: Digital.

Anchorman: The Legend of Ron Burgundy
Unprinted / personal work

LOCATION Beavercreek, Ohio / US

SITE Adamlimbert.com

BEHIND THE POSTER: *Anchorman* is, by far, one of my favorite comedies of all time. I would say it holds the #2 spot on my top ten list. It's one of those "tent pole" comedies that has really influenced a generation. Me included. An amazing job from all involved: McKay, Ferrell, Rudd, all of them, they're all geniuses.

INFLUENCES: I'm influenced by all different types of art. From comic illustration and cartooning to graphic design and filmmaking to music and tattoo art. Here is a list of some great people doing great things: Hydro74, Ashley Wood, Olivier Coipel, Jim Cheung, Nikko Hurtado, Kris Anka, Olly Moss, Invisible Creature, Brandon Rike, Tom Whalen. The list could seriously go on forever.

FAVORITE FILM / GENRE: Another tough one. I *love* movies! Love them. I don't know that I have a favorite genre. I'm just a fan of good movies. And trying to choose my absolute favorite is near impossible. But here's a clichéd yet truthful answer: *Pulp Fiction*.

FIRST FILM: *E.T.*, I think.

PREFERRED MEDIUM: Three things I love to throw around are pencils, inks, and vectors.

ADDITIONAL REMARKS: Stay fierce.

The Naked Gun: From the Files of Police Squad!
27 × 40 in (69 × 102 cm)

DESIGN FIRM	Wing's Art & Design Studio
LOCATION	Somerset / UK
SITE	Wingsart.net

BEHIND THE POSTER: I'm drawn to interesting faces, and Leslie Nielsen had a great, cartoonish face full of expression. The *Naked Gun, Airplane,* and *Hot Shot* movies were all deadpan slapstick, and Nielsen was the master at it. Also, the fan poster scene is dominated by horror films, so I wanted to add something a bit different.

FIRST FILM: When I was a kid, we had Friday video nights where we'd watch whatever Dad brought home for the weekend. I have vivid memories of watching *Rambo* and loving it. Other nights included a healthy mixture of *Poltergeist, The Goonies,* and *Return of the Living Dead*. I'll also never forget my teenage embarrassment of watching *Basic Instinct* with my parents. Utter torture.

PREFERRED MEDIUM: Simple, black-ink line work. It's an unforgiving medium, but incredibly satisfying when you get it right.

ADDITIONAL REMARKS: The movie poster business is in an odd state. The marketing man considers good art too retro and confusing for the consumer, only to replace it with depressing and indistinguishable Photoshop disasters. Marketers should remember that quality poster art speaks to our imaginations, and this is a much more powerful tool than going straight for the wallet.

BEHIND THE POSTERS: The *Killer Klowns* and *The Evil Dead* movie posters were commissions for the Florida-based horror convention Spooky Empire.

INFLUENCES: Vaughn Bode, Sam Kieth, Jack Davis, and all of *Mad* magazine's original, usual gang of idiots. Film directors: Jean-Pierre Jeunet, Sam Raimi, Dario Argento.

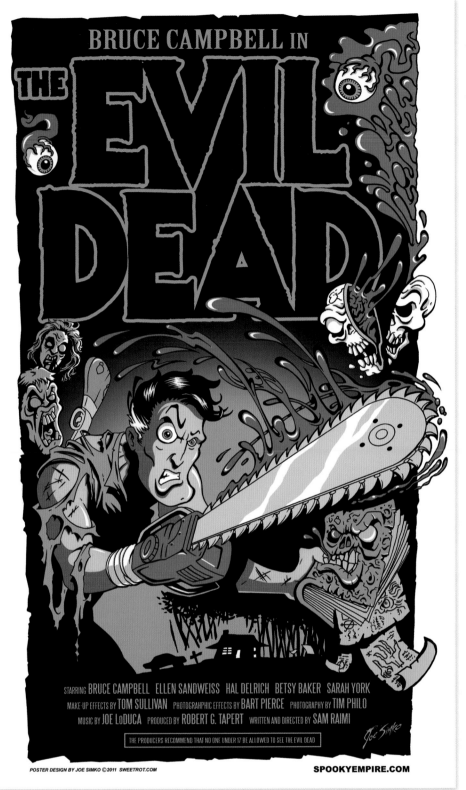

The Evil Dead
14 x 23 in (36 x 58 cm)

LOCATION New York, New York / US
SITE Joesimko.com + Wax-eye.com

FAVORITE FILM / GENRE: Hard to choose a favorite film, but my favorite genres of film are horror and comedy.
FIRST FILM: First film I saw in the theater was *The Great Muppet Caper.*

PREFERRED MEDIUM: Acrylic paints, inks.

A film by Joel & Ethan Coen

Starring   William H. Macy   Steve Buscemi   Frances McDormand   Peter Stormare

Continued from page 89

BEHIND THE POSTER: *Fargo* was a personal piece. I've always been a fan of simple designs and grids, so this was one of my early experiments, trying to do typography with other elements, in this case snowflakes and drops of blood, which I thought were a fitting theme for the movie. I still remember organizing and moving around all the hundreds of snowflakes into position, and making it look like an irregular pattern. It was very time consuming, and I got dizzy zooming in on all the snowflakes.

THANK YOU FOR SMOKING

Thank You for Smoking
12 × 17 in (30 × 42 cm - A3)

BEHIND THE POSTER: I love the theme of this movie, the balance between morality and profit, and the question of "what is bad?"
INFLUENCES: Socialist propaganda and Polish film posters.

FAVORITE FILM / GENRE: I love drama/comedy, as well as cult films.
FIRST FILM: *Sinbad and the Eye of the Tiger* (1977).
PREFERRED MEDIUM: Profit and death.

Garrett Ross

The Prestige
Unprinted / personal work

DESIGN FIRM Grafik Design
LOCATION Los Angeles, California / US
SITE Grafik.net

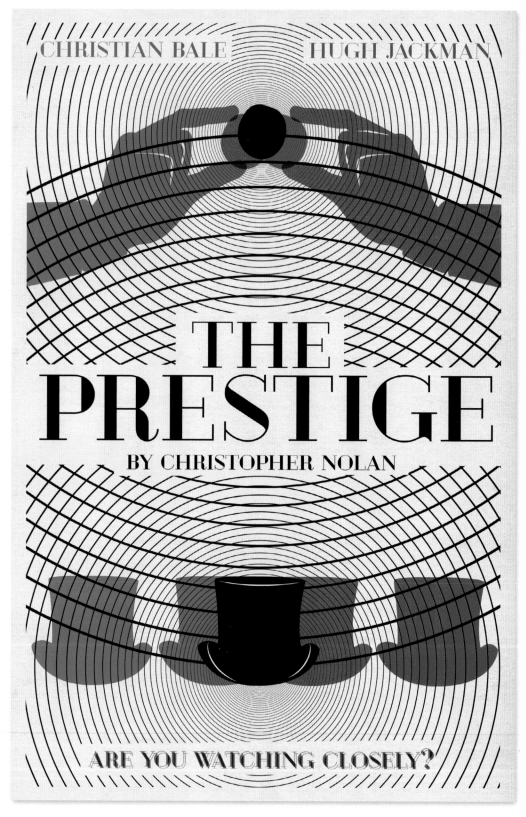

CHRISTIAN BALE   HUGH JACKMAN

THE PRESTIGE
BY CHRISTOPHER NOLAN

ARE YOU WATCHING CLOSELY?

BEHIND THE POSTER: I loved how much of the story in *The Prestige* was represented with simple, minimal imagery: the shot of all the top hats on the ground, all the light bulbs, the birdcage optical illusion, the bouncing ball. I wanted to do something with the symmetry in the characters and connect it to the art style of the setting.

INFLUENCES: Jay Shaw, Olly Moss, Paul Pope, Kevin Tong, DKNG.

FAVORITE FILM / GENRE: Science-fiction.
FIRST FILM: *Return of the Jedi.*
ADDITIONAL REMARKS: The alternative movie poster scene (and my dip into it) were huge in my artistic career. I landed a lot of my initial (and most important) jobs from placing these posters into my profile.

BE AFRAID. BE VERY AFRAID.

JEFF GOLDBLUM

A DAVID CRONENBERG FILM

THE FLY

with GEENA DAVIS JOHN GETZ music by HOWARD SHORE
SCREENPLAY by CHARLES EDWARD POGUE and DAVID CRONENBERG
PRODUCED by STUART CORNFIELD DIRECTED by DAVID CRONENBERG

The Fly
18 x 24 in (46 x 61 cm)

Fernando Reza

DESIGN FIRM	Frodesignco.
LOCATION	Los Angeles, California / US
SITE	Frodesignco.com

BEHIND THE POSTER: This print was part of the CHUD Salutes series. CHUD is an online, film news site. We linked up to pay tribute to films that we love. *The Fly* is an unapologetic genre movie. It is an old Cineplex, mom and pop video store, poor quality VHS, movie. It reminds me of a certain type of film from the '50s—cold war films, atomic sci-fi films. At its core it warns against industrialization and rampant technology changing the world in ways that could be dangerous and irrevocable. Plus it's just very entertaining, cheesy horror effects and all.
INFLUENCES: *Twilight Zone*, Andy Kaufman, and rock and roll music.

FAVORITE FILM / GENRE: I love surreal films. Fellini, Bunuel, and Emir Kustarica.
ADDITIONAL REMARKS: As part of the CHUD Salutes series, we've done 18 posters so far, ranging from *The Shining* to *Godzilla vs. Biollante*. Additionally, I work regularly with Gallery 1988 (Los Angeles), Spoke Art (San Francisco), and Bottleneck Gallery (New York). I've also designed alternative posters for Troma studios and contributed to marketing campaigns for *The Cabin in the Woods, Super 8,* and *Chronicle.*

L'uccello dalle piume di cristallo
20 × 28 in (51 × 70 cm)

LOCATION Tortona / Italy

SITE Malleusdelic.com

BEHIND THE POSTERS: We were contacted by the Dark City Gallery in the UK to create a poster series dedicated to Dario Argento's films. We worked on nine prints, each with a standard version and one variation.

INFLUENCES: Malleus is a three headed Cerberus, so there are too many influences to list. However, our main, shared inspiration is surely the beauty of women.
PREFERRED MEDIUM: Handmade silkscreen.

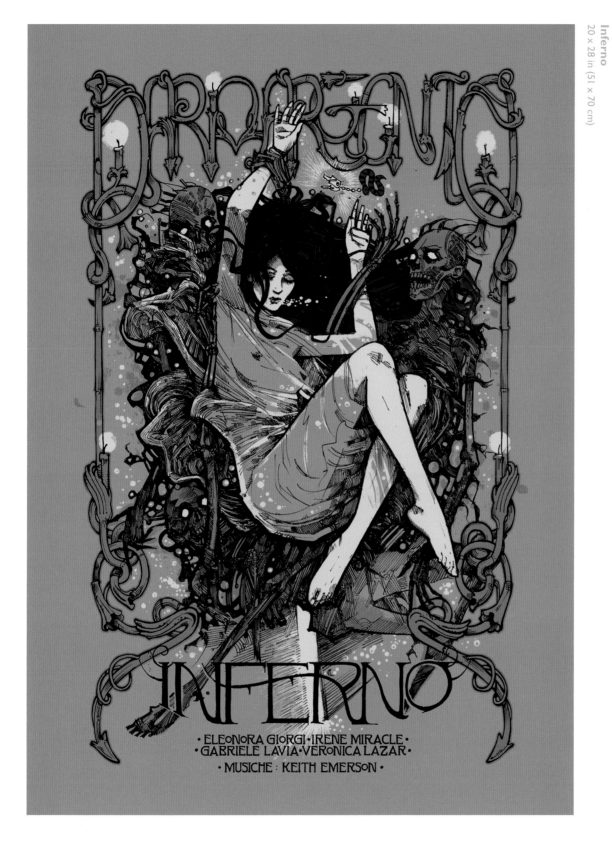

LOCATION Tortona / Italy
SITE Malleusdelic.com

Johnny Destructo

LOCATION Philadelphia, Pennsylvania / US

SITE Jaydotdee.com + Johnnydestructo.com

Poltergeist
11 x 17 in (28 × 43 cm)

THE COLONIAL THEATRE PRESENTS

POLTERGEIST

AUGUST THIRD. FIRST FRIDAY FRIGHT NIGHTS. WWW.COLONIALTHEATRE.COM

BEHIND THE POSTER: A local theater [The Colonial in Phoenixville, Pennsylvania] shows original prints of classic and cult films, and I'm one of the lucky artists that they've tapped to produce posters for their events.

INFLUENCES: Tara McPherson, Becky Cloonan, J. Scott Campbell, Jordan Crane, and Dave Johnson are some of my favorite illustrators. Favorite film directors would have to be Quentin Tarantino and Edgar Wright. Graphic designers: Chip Kidd and Saul Bass.

FAVORITE FILM / GENRE: *Fight Club*, but my favorite genre is horror. I think that I spend the most time watching a variety of horror films, from slow-build Asian horror to straight-up splatter porn (it's a thing, look it up).

FIRST FILM: My earliest memory of a movie theater experience has to be *Return of the Jedi* in 1984. I was 6, and it was *the all*.

PREFERRED MEDIUM: I usually sketch ideas out in pencil, take a pic of it with my iPhone, and then finish everything else in Photoshop using the miraculous Wacom 21UX monitor. I...I love that thing, like an uncomfortable amount for a human to love something that isn't programmed to love back.

Videodrome
40 × 30 in (102 × 76 cm - Quad)

CIGARETTE BURNS PRESENTS

VIDEODROME

FILM 11.30PM / DJ AND BAR UNTIL 2.30AM | SATURDAY OCTOBER 22 | RIO DALSTON | £7.50

RIO CINEMA 107 KINGSLAND HIGH STREET LONDON E8 2PB TEL 020 7241 9410 RIOCINEMA.ORG.UK CIGARETTEBURNSCINEMA.COM

ALIAS	Creative Output
LOCATION	London / UK
SITE	Creative-output.co.uk + OTMentertain.com

BEHIND THE POSTER: I'm good friends with Josh Saco, who runs the cult film night Cigarette Burns at the Rio in Dalston, London. He gets in touch from time to time with some awesome films that he needs art for. *Videodrome* is a Cronenberg classic that I've seen a fair number of times.

INFLUENCES: Visually, directors like Fincher, Hitchcock, Ford, Kubrick, Mallick, and Spielberg really inspire me.

FIRST FILM: I had a roster of films that I would watch regularly as a kid: *Superman*, *Raiders of the Lost Ark*, *E.T.*, *Star Wars*, the usual for that time. But as a child of the Betamax age, and having a lack of BBFC enforcement in the house, I was also watching *Rambo*, *A Nightmare on Elm Street*, and *Carrie* [BBFC is equivalent to the Motion Picture Association of America ratings]. So this probably warped my world view and fired my creativity early on.

PREFERRED MEDIUM: After spending years working digitally, I find it great to get back to the basics—I just love screen printing. It feels honest.

LOCATION Toronto, Ontario / Canada

SITE Inkjava.com + Lezardfrileux.blogspot.com

BEHIND THE POSTERS: These illustrations were made for an art show at a comic book shop in Ottawa. *Sleepy Hollow* is among my favorites from Tim Burton, and I find Chucky [right] pretty amiable among the serial killer bunch.

INFLUENCES: I feel like I always have two tiny masters over my shoulders when I draw: one is Bruce Timm, the other is Tim Burton. I cling to Bruce Timm's style for its clean look and angular style, and I like Burton's grittiness and how he dares to explore very dark subjects through the eye of a child. I think they both transpire in my work through my lines and the point of view. I also have a deep fondness over everything from French director Jean-Pierre Jeunet. His movies are a feast for the eyes, making terrific use of colors and shot angles.

Child's Play 2
13 x 18 in (33 x 46 cm)

SORRY JACK...CHUCKY'S BACK!

CHILD'S PLAY 2

LOCATION Toronto, Ontario / Canada

SITE Inkjava.com + Lezardfrileux.blogspot.com

FAVORITE FILM / GENRE: I always had a predilection for sci-fi/horror/fantasy material and it comes from the fact that these are such dramatic genres, always very flamboyant and strongly flavored. There's so much creativity within these genres, and it gives one the freedom to explore imaginary worlds.

My favorite movie without a doubt is *Alien Resurrection*. Jeunet made it the biggest piece of eye candy of the whole franchise, with Sigourney Weaver more mesmerizing than ever as a fierce new Ripley. And the movie's Poseidon Adventure-in-space plot is just pure fun.

FIRST FILM: Very, very first? *The Little Mermaid*. Over and over again.

PREFERRED MEDIUM: For my own pleasure, pencil and paper. I would add markers and pen to that, but fundamentally that's all I need to enjoy drawing. However, for professional reasons I do like to make use of my graphic tablet because it's more convenient to edit, share, and make prints afterwards.

Ale Giorgini

LOCATION Vicenza / Italy

SITE Alegiorgini.com

The Big Lebowski
26 x 40 in (66 x 102 cm)

INFLUENCES: I love vintage cartoons. When I was child I watched Hanna-Barbera cartoons all day, and today I admire artists with a similar style, including Tartakovsky, Derek Yaniger, Shag, and many more. I am influenced by film directors as well: Tarantino, Burton, The Coen Brothers, Hitchcock, and George Lucas are some of my favorites.

FAVORITE FILM / GENRE: When I was a teenager I was addicted to horror and sci-fi films. My collection of posters, VHS videos, and DVDs is still at my parents' house.

Back to the Future
26 x 40 in (66 x 102 cm)

▼ Ale Giorgini

LOCATION Vicenza / Italy
SITE Alegiorgini.com

FIRST FILM: In the theaters it was *Ghostbusters*. I still love that one.
PREFERRED MEDIUM: I sketch my designs with pencil and then move to Adobe Illustrator.

ADDITIONAL REMARKS: I love films and that's why I design posters. I was thrilled recently (early 2013) when The Oscars recommended my art on their site. I also enjoy television and I am in the process of designing some celebratory show posters. As I am writing this, I am working on a poster for *The Walking Dead*.

The Hitcher
24 × 36 in (61 × 91 cm)

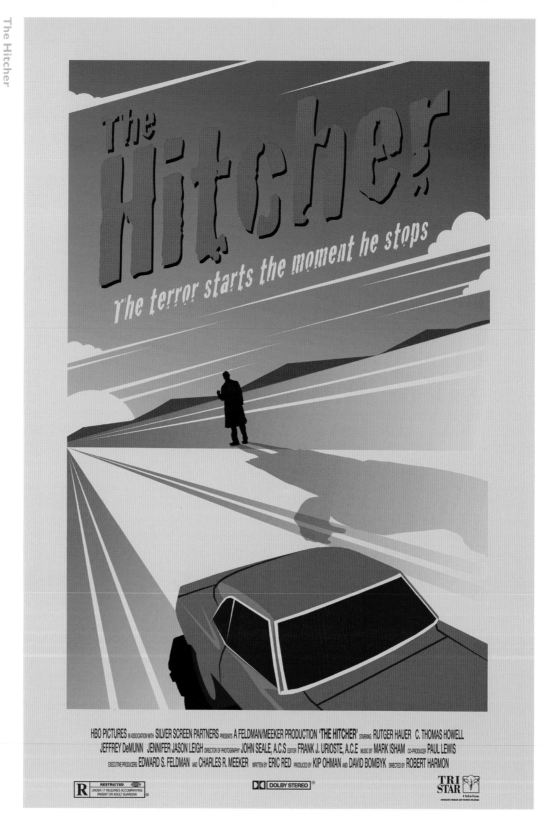

BEHIND THE POSTERS: I wanted to create a set of retro road movie posters using minimal design and a minimal color palette. I made a list of some of the classic all-time road movies: *Easy Rider*, *Duel*, *The Hitcher*, and, of course, *Vanishing Point* [right], probably the ultimate road movie. The designs were no-brainers. I knew that they had to be in linear perspective and incorporate actual vanishing points.

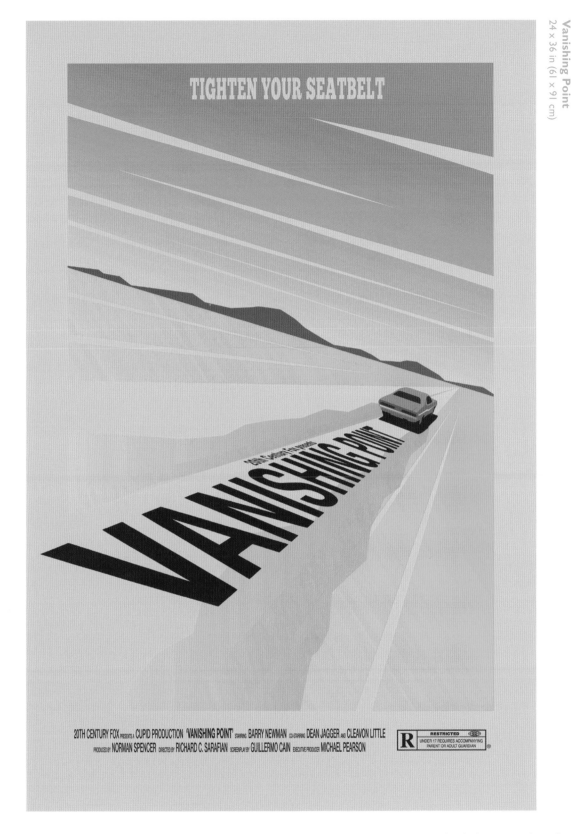

LOCATION Scotland

SITE Ollieboyd.com + Society6.com/ollieboyd

INFLUENCES: Saul Bass, Tom Whalen, Janee Meadows (I love how her style is so diverse), Tyler Stout, Olly Moss.
FAVORITE FILM / GENRE: Sci-fi. Visually I thought *Tron: Legacy* was one of the most stunning movies of recent years.

FIRST FILM: I think that it may have been *Superman* (1978).
PREFERRED MEDIUM: Digital (Illustrator and Photoshop).

LOCATION Newcastle / UK

SITE Oldredjalopy.com + Oldredjalopy-blog.com

Star Wars: Episode IV – A New Hope

17 x 23 in (42 x 59 cm - A2)

BEHIND THE POSTERS: I think everybody my age has been affected by *Star Wars*, directly or indirectly. It was a huge cultural touchstone and constantly inspires fan art of all types. Its broad social appeal makes it much easier to play with than other similar movies. You can have fun with the subject and know that most people, even those who don't know *Star Wars* all that well, will understand the humor.

I was seeing a lot of minimalist posters for *Star Wars* and wanted to create something more intricate that wasn't just a straight montage or character portrait. The fight poster style allowed me to engage the viewer, to make them look past the initial design and see additional details (which is also where I can build the humorous elements).

INFLUENCES: Long before I even knew who he was I was influenced by Drew Struzan. I remember trying to emulate his style in my own drawings as I was growing up, especially his posters for *Indiana Jones and the Last Crusade* and *Hook*.

In a similar vein, I love the paintings of Hugh Fleming, another fantastic *Star Wars* artist. I also love the vector illustration work of Jessica Finson, and am in awe of the fantastic digital illustration style of Patrick Brown.

FAVORITE FILM / GENRE: I'm a big fan of the Korean film industry and particularly Park Chan-Wook. *Oldboy* is definitely one of my favorite films.

FIRST FILM: Probably Spielberg's *E.T.* I went to see it twice. However, the first movie to have a really big impact on me was *Return of the Jedi.* I remember being obsessed with it. I became famous in the playground for my drawings of Stormtroopers!

PREFERRED MEDIUM: I started out as a freehand artist, pens and pencils. Once I found my way to a university, I discovered Photoshop, Illustrator, and FreeHand. Since then, I've almost exclusively worked with digital. I often begin my ideas in a sketchbook, but they ultimately end up being digital.

Chris Thornley

The Bourne Legacy
Unprinted / personal work

ALIAS	Raid7I
LOCATION	Darwen / UK
SITE	Raid7I.com

Continued from page 72

BEHIND THE POSTER: *Bourne Legacy* was a commission to help promote the release of the film in the UK. The art appeared in various magazines.

The Dark Knight Rises
11 x 17 in (28 x 43 cm)

A CHRISTOPHER NOLAN FILM

THE DARK KNIGHT RISES

CHRISTIAN BALE · TOM HARDY · ANNE HATHAWAY

GARY OLDMAN · MICHAEL CAINE · JOSEPH GORDON-LEVITT · MORGAN FREEMAN

BEHIND THE POSTER: I consider myself one of *Batman*'s biggest fans, especially *Batman* from the "Nolanverse." His [Christopher Nolan's] trilogy was amazing. Ever since the public received the first official photo of Tom Hardy as Bane I had to create my own poster for the movie.

INFLUENCES: Christopher Nolan (of course), Neville Brody (graphic designer), Martin Scorsese, Quentin Tarantino, Ridley Scott, the Wachowski brothers and Drew Struzan.

FAVORITE FILM / GENRE: Comic book films, period pieces, mafia.

FIRST FILM: I remember seeing *Teenage Mutant Ninja Turtles* in the theatre as a very young child. It was my first time being in a movie theatre. This was in my home country of Jamaica, but they showed it about two years after it premiered in the US.

PREFERRED MEDIUM: Pencil, ink, and paper.

Continued from page 37

BEHIND THE POSTERS: For me, the *Friday the 13th* film series spans a particularly fun period for horror. During the '80s, several horror franchises went from straight horror to parody in only a few films. *Friday the 13th* is one of the worst (best) offenders.

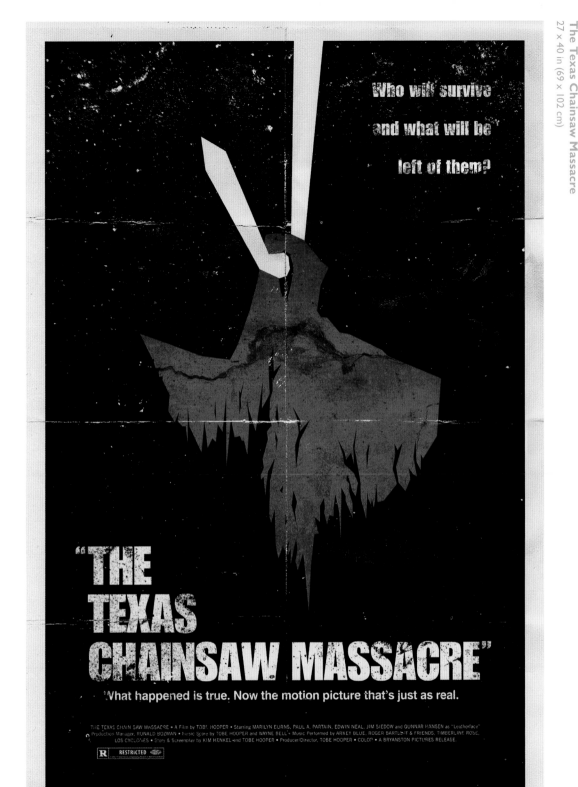

Also, watching *The Texas Chainsaw Massacre* for the first time is one of my fondest film memories. I was at a friend's house and we watched it late at night, and I was just stunned at how terrifying it was. As soon as it ended, he started *Texas Chainsaw Massacre 2*, and I was equally stunned at how hilarious it was.

James Gilleard

King Kong
17 × 23 in (42 × 59 cm - A2)
A Three Barrels, Ltd. release

DESIGN FIRM | James Gilleard Illustration and Animation
LOCATION | London / UK
SITE | jamesgilleard.com

BEHIND THE POSTERS: *King Kong* was created for Three Barrels, Ltd. and all of the proceeds went to charity. I loved this film as a child, and even the new version (2005) is great escapist cinema on first viewing in the cinema.

The Creature from the Black Lagoon [right] was a different situation. I was working for a company that was changing management (from bad to worse!) and the artists had some down time. This meant that we could work on anything we wanted to during the day. I think I spent about three days on this piece! I love old B movies and have a big collection at home, so this was a poster that I wanted to create for a while.

INFLUENCES: In terms of Illustration artists, I love the work of Charlie Harper. He had a completely unique mid-century minimalist style that I mistook for vector artwork when I first saw it. I also enjoy the work of Alain Gree, Robert Mcguinness, Glenn Barr, Sanjay Patel, Chris Ware, Dave Cooper, Ragnar, and many others. Cartoons influence me as well, from Disney classics to the Warner Brothers Looney Toons and Hanna-Barbera to the UPA style.

James Gilleard

DESIGN FIRM	James Gilleard Illustration and Animation
LOCATION	London / UK
SITE	jamesgilleard.com

FAVORITE FILM / GENRE: Comedies and animated films. Wes Anderson is my favorite director—his films are completely unique, funny and with heart. *The Life Aquatic with Steve Zissou* is just unbelievably good.

FIRST FILM: The scary films stick with me. I remember hiding behind a cushion watching *Jaws*, and being so insanely scared of *Alien*.

PREFERRED MEDIUM: My work tends to be digital and is mostly created in Illustrator. I drew quite realistic art growing up, with traditional mediums such as watercolors, acrylics, and oil painting as well as graphite pencil drawings and sketches. My work still has a strong grounding in traditional media before moving it into the computer. I find it impossible to begin new pieces in Illustrator or Photoshop without first sketching them on paper.

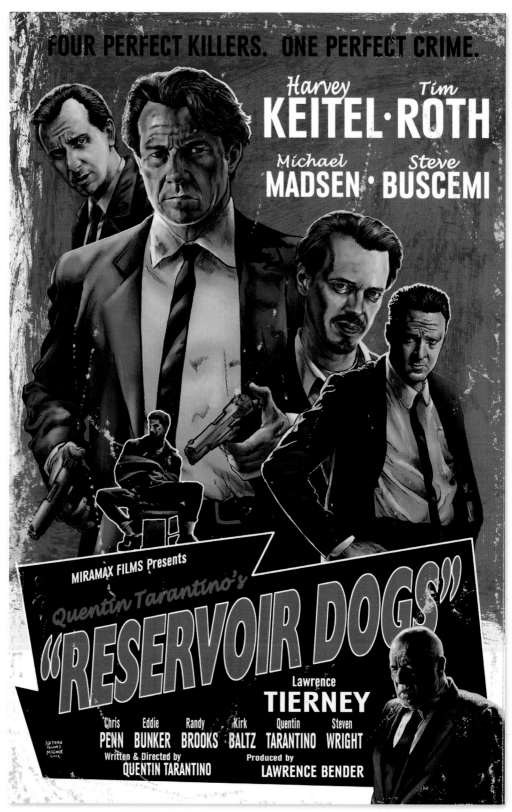
BEHIND THE POSTERS: I chose *Reservoir Dogs* because it is my second favorite movie of all time. I had already created a poster for *Reservoir Dogs* years earlier, but felt that it was time for a new version. *The Terminator* poster [right] came about for HorrorHound Weekend. I work for *HorrorHound Magazine* and in September '12, the magazine held a convention in Indianapolis that featured a *Terminator* reunion; I created this poster for the event. I am a big fan of the film and always felt that it was very similar to '80s slasher flicks, so I wanted to do a slasher film-inspired movie poster.

INFLUENCES: I started out in comics, but my passion is film, so my influences are across the board. Artists like Frank Frazetta, Berni Wrightson, Jim Lee, Alex Ross, and Brian Bolland. Directors: Quentin Tarantino, Richard Linklater, Martin Scorsese, Sergio Leone, Sam Peckinpah, John Woo, David Fincher, and more.
FAVORITE FILM / GENRE: My all-time favorite film is *Taxi Driver*. It's the perfect storm of three of the most talented filmmakers (Robert De Niro, Martin Scorsese, and Paul Schrader) all coming together at the same time, totally hungry and wanting to show the world what they could do.

IT CAN'T BE BARGAINED WITH.
IT CAN'T BE REASONED WITH.
IT DOESN'T FEEL PITY, REMORSE,
OR FEAR.

AND IT ABSOLUTELY WILL
NOT STOP....EVER...
UNTIL YOU ARE
DEAD

THE TERMINATOR

HEMDALE PRESENTS A PACIFIC WESTERN PRODUCTION OF A JAMES CAMERON FILM
ARNOLD SCHWARZENEGGER "THE TERMINATOR" MICHAEL BIEHN LINDA HAMILTON LANCE HENRIKSEN and PAUL WINFIELD
Make-up FX by STAN WINSTON Executive Producers JOHN DALY & DEREK GIBSON
Written & Directed by JAMES CAMERON with GALE ANNE HURD Produced by GALE ANNE HURD
Directed by JAMES CAMERON

The Terminator
11 x 17 in (28 x 43 cm)

Nathan Thomas Milliner

COMPANIES Rebel Rouser Comics, LLC / HorrorHound Magazine
LOCATION Louisville, Kentucky / US
SITE Rebelrouserart.com

PREFERRED MEDIUM: I love inking. I am most happy sitting down with a sheet of paper and an ink pen (I use Micron pens) in my hand. When I became a published artist, I played around with Photoshop to learn how to paint. It's still a work in progress for me.
ADDITIONAL REMARKS: For the first 100 years of cinema, original artwork was used to promote films and there was nothing like walking into the lobby of a movie house and seeing beautifully illustrated movie posters from Drew Struzan and other artists. Or, walking into the video store and seeing rows of VHS cover art. Great art could make the worst of movies appealing to the viewer.

There is a great desire from fans to return to this, and to have a book filled with artists doing their artistic interpretations of movie posters is something that I'm very proud to be a part of. I look forward to having this on my bookshelf.

Mean Girls
9 x 15 in (23 x 38 cm)

Mitch Ansara

ALIAS	Spacesick
LOCATION	Toledo, Ohio / US
SITE	Spacesick.com

BEHIND THE POSTERS: I love *Mean Girls* and *Sixteen Candles* more than a fat kid loves cake made out of rainbows and smiles. And although I was never a love-struck teenage redhead like the films' heroines, the awkward high schooler in me will treasure both of these classics for as long as I live. Like the rest of my *I Can Read Movies* series, I chose them because they just happened to be the particular movies I wanted to watch those days. Letting them play while I drew was just another excuse to watch 'em again. "She doesn't even GO here!"

INFLUENCES: Even though I don't come close to their level, some of my biggest influences are Chuck Jones' fun animated characters, the striking graphic art of Saul Bass, and the fantasy worlds and beautiful ladies of Frank Frazetta.

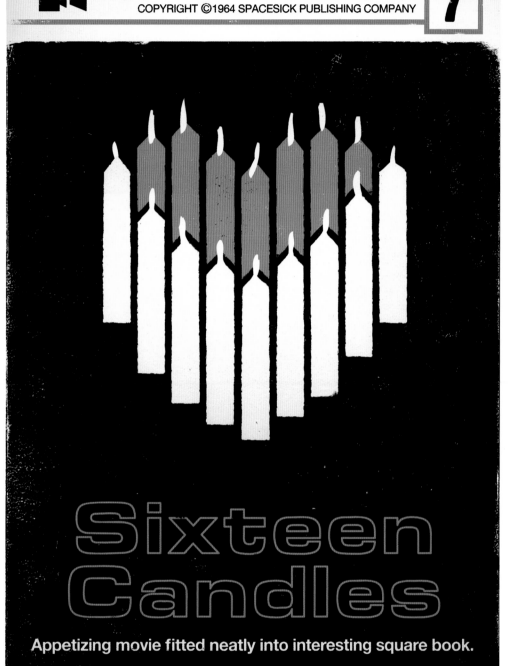

Part of the "I Can Read Movies" Series

COPYRIGHT ©1964 SPACESICK PUBLISHING COMPANY

Book

7

Sixteen Candles
9 x 15 in (23 x 38 cm)

Sixteen Candles

Appetizing movie fitted neatly into interesting square book.

▼ **Mitch Ansara**

ALIAS	Spacesick
LOCATION	Toledo, Ohio / US
SITE	Spacesick.com

FAVORITE FILM / GENRE: *Ghostbusters* is my favorite movie of all time, and I *never* miss a chance to see it in the theater! Though all the '80s kids movies and comedies I watched over and over again as a kid will always be close to my heart.

PREFERRED MEDIUM: Digital.

More artwork from Mitch Ansara on page 160

ALIAS	Spacesick
LOCATION	Toledo, Ohio / US
SITE	Spacesick.com

Continued from page 159

BEHIND THE POSTER: Alamo Drafthouse asked me to create a poster for the event. I love '70s schlock.

LOCATION	Berlin / Germany
SITE	Malatesta.mysupadupa.com

Continued from page 101

BEHIND THE POSTER: *Raging Bull* is one of my favorite movies. I grew up watching the films of De Niro—he is one of my idols. De Niro's interpretation of his character in *Raging Bull* is perfection, for example, gaining 30 kilos to get into the boxer's old and decadent phase. Are there still examples of actors so pure?

Star Wars: Episode II – Attack of the Clones
11 x 17 in (28 x 43 cm)

ALIAS   akaStarWarskid
LOCATION   Austin, Texas / US
SITE   Akastarwarskid.tumblr.com
             + Hipster-movie-posters.tumblr.com

BEHIND THE POSTERS: *Attack of the Clones* holds a special place for me (I'm a diehard *Star Wars* fan if the nickname didn't give it away). The scope of *Episode II* rocked my world. I felt so small in the universe. Not just as a human being, but as an artist. I was just getting into making my own films, and when *AOTC* came out, the bar that I was reaching for went even higher. People talk smack about the prequels, but honestly, when was the last time they dreamt up entire universes and then created them for the whole world to experience?

Also, through all the hype of the superhero genre, I think *Batman* [right] stands the test of time because he has a closer basis to reality, and as hopeless as Gotham may be, Bruce never gives up on her.

INFLUENCES: In regards to my love for *Star Wars*, George Lucas is a huge role model. He did more than just write and direct hugely successful sci-fi movies, he created an empire. He started from scratch and didn't play by the rules. Lucas is an artist who settles for no less than his vision, and I admire that.

One of my other influences was Saul Bass. As an artist and designer, Bass took the commercial and made it his own. What I admire most about his work is its depth. While Bass' work is considered minimalism, the imagery he created did more. The visuals of his art conjured up the heart of the subject. His movie posters often only consisted of three or four colors, but that man put them to work.

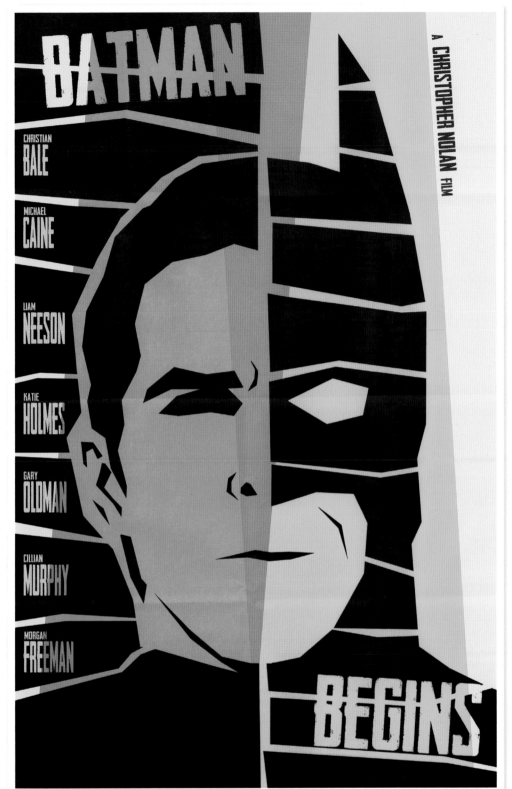

Batman Begins
11 x 17 in (28 x 43 cm)

ALIAS	akaStarWarskid
LOCATION	Austin, Texas / US
SITE	Akastarwarskid.tumblr.com + Hipster-movie-posters.tumblr.com

FIRST FILM: *Return of the Jedi.* It's not the first film that I remember seeing, but at age four, it's certainly the one that made the biggest impression.

PREFERRED MEDIUM: For the majority of my art, I go digital, but from time to time, I like to try mixed media. Those are usually the pieces that end up on my own walls or that I give to my friends and family.

ADDITIONAL REMARKS: Seek to entertain. Dare to provoke.

More artwork from Travis English on pages 188 and 189

DESIGN FIRM Needle Design

LOCATION Cardiff, Wales / UK (originally from Oxford, UK)

SITE Mattneedle.co.uk + Needledesign.bigcartel.com

BEHIND THE POSTER: I was asked to design the *Moonrise Kingdom* print for a *ShortList* magazine feature. I'm a fan of *Moonrise Kingdom* and all of Wes Anderson's films.

INFLUENCES: My main inspirations include Andy Warhol, Drew Struzan, Ralph Steadman, Saul Bass, Milton Glaser, Dali, Edward Hopper, Wes Anderson, Alfred Hitchcock, Stanley Kubrick, Terry Gilliam, Bauhaus, and Roman Cieślewicz.

FAVORITE FILM / GENRE: *North by Northwest, Into the Wild, Adaptation, Drive, The Royal Tenenbaums,* and *The Godfather* are a few of my favorite films.

FIRST FILM: Probably Disney's *Fantasia.* I had no idea what was happening, but I loved all of the colors, shapes, and sounds. I now own it on DVD 25 years later...and I still have no idea what's going on.

PREFERRED MEDIUM: My work used to be much more experimental. When I started out, I combined collage, hand-drawn images, and vector with strong typographical elements. Now I bring all of these elements together to create my own style/approach.

Hard Eight
10 x 14 in (25 x 36 cm)

Philip Baker Hall
a Paul Thomas Anderson *picture*

HARD
8

RYSHER ENTERTAINMENT PRESENTS A GREEN PARROT PRODUCTION IN ASSOCIATION WITH TRINITY
A PT.ANDERSON PICTURE "HARD EIGHT" MUSIC BY MICHAEL PENN AND JON BRION
COSTUME DESIGNER MARK BRIDGES EDITOR BARBARA TULLIVER PRODUCTION DESIGNER NANCY DEREN
EXECUTIVE PRODUCERS KEITH SAMPLES HANS BROCKMANN FRANÇOIS DUPLAT
PRODUCERS DANIEL LUPI PRODUCED BY ROBERT JONES JOHN LYONS DIRECTOR OF PHOTOGRAPHY ROBERT ELSWIT
WRITTEN AND DIRECTED BY PAUL THOMAS ANDERSON

mr-Bluebird

LOCATION Pasadena, California / US (originally from Brazil)
SITE Mr-bluebird.deviantart.com + Mario-graciotti.tumblr.com

BEHIND THE POSTER: Paul Thomas Anderson is my favorite director, so I wanted to make a series of posters for his films.
INFLUENCES: I love the aesthetics of the '60s. Be it from illustrations, movies, furniture, architecture, etc. As for specific artists, I'm a huge fan of Mary Blair, Eyvind Earle, Rolly Crump, Charley Harper, and Chris Ware.

FAVORITE FILM / GENRE: All of Paul Thomas Anderson's films are among my favorites. I also love *Brazil, 2001: A Space Odyssey, Mulholland Drive,* and *Ratatouille,* among many others.
PREFERRED MEDIUM: Pen/paper and digital coloring. Vectors as well.

The DaVinci Code
28 x 32 in (71 x 81 cm)

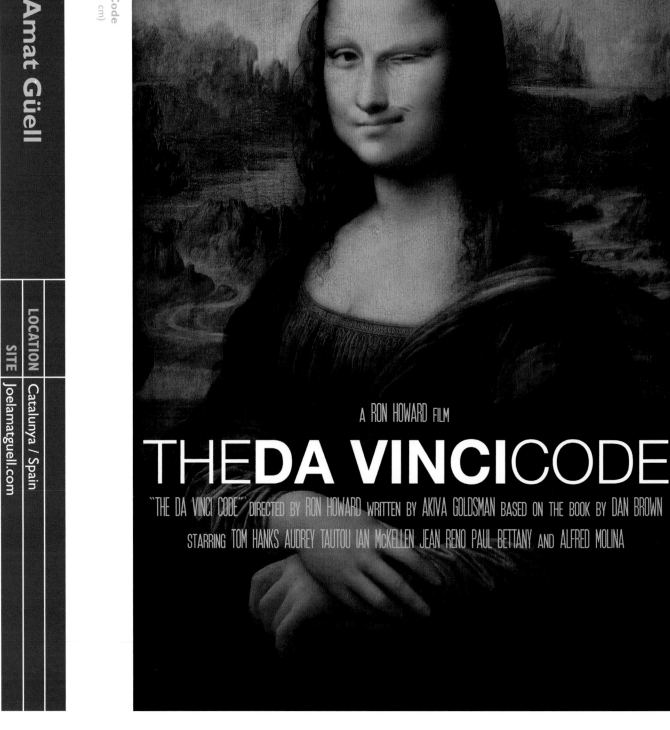

LOCATION Catalunya / Spain

SITE joelamatguell.com

Continued from page 76

LOCATION London / UK

SITE Alexbutenko.co.uk

RISE OF THE APES

TWENTIETH CENTURY FOX AND CHERNIN ENTERTAINMENT PRESENT A FILM BY RUPERT WYATT JAMES FRANCO FRIDA PINTO BRIAN COX AND ANDY SERKINS "RISE OF THE APES"
TOM FELTON TYLER LABINE JOHN LITHGOW DAVID HEWLETT SNOJA BENNETT JAMIE HARRIS DAVID OYELOWO CHELAH HORSDAL LEAH GIBSON MONICA MUSTELIER KARIN KONOVAL
PRODUCED BY AMANDA SILVER RICK JAFFA PETER CHERNIN AND DYLAN CLARK MUSIC BY PATRICK DOYLE CINEMATOGRAPHY ANDREW LESNIE EDITED CONRAD BUFF AND MARK GOLDBLATT
SCREENPLAY AMANDA SILVER RICK JAFFA AND JAMIE MOSS DIRECTED BY RUPERT WYATT

NOVEMBER 2011

BEHIND THE POSTER: In 2010, 20th Century Fox enlisted students to create marketing campaigns for *Rise of the Apes,* and this was my submission. The core idea for the poster was to replace an image of a human being in an iconic work of religious art with that of an ape, suggesting the rise of apes above humanity. I created posters based on *The Last Supper* and *The Creation of Adam* [shown here], which is my favorite. The iconic bit of the Sistine Chapel, which I have edited by replacing Adam's hand with that of an ape's, questions the superiority of human beings above other species.

INFLUENCES: I look to a lot of Russian constructivism and contemporary collage artists. Regarding movie posters, I find inspiration in the works of the Stenberg brothers and Bill Gold.
FAVORITE FILM / GENRE: *The Dark Knight.*
FIRST FILM: The very first films that I remember watching were '60s Soviet comedies. There was something very special about the humor in those films—it was beautiful satire filled with self-irony.
PREFERRED MEDIUM: I prefer working with handmade media, such as collages, and then editing them digitally.

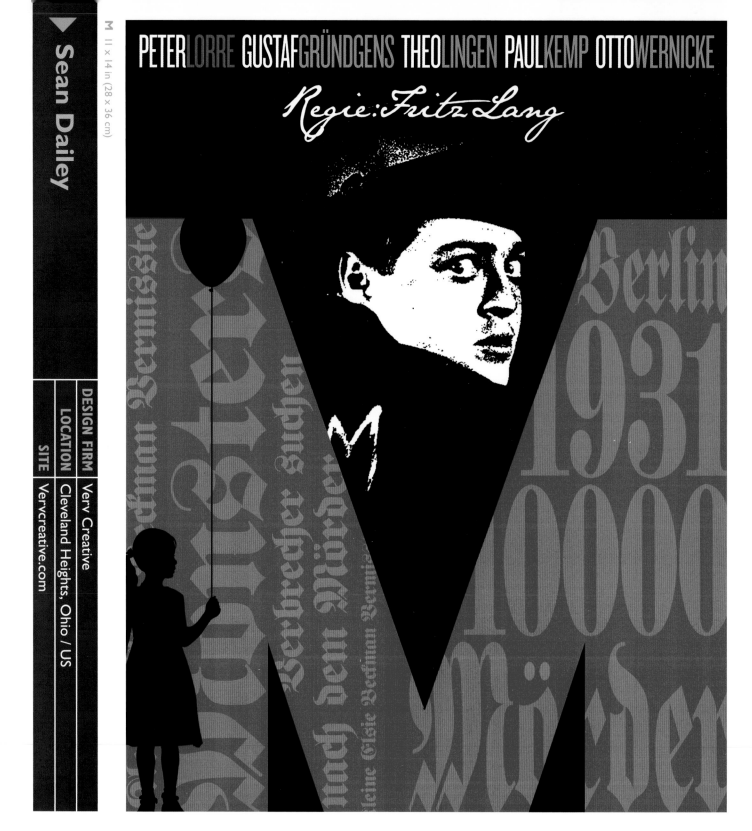

Sean Dailey

M 11 x 14 in (28 x 36 cm)

DESIGN FIRM Verv Creative

LOCATION Cleveland Heights, Ohio / US

SITE Vervcreative.com

PETERLORRE GUSTAFGRÜNDGENS THEOLINGEN PAULKEMP OTTOWERNICKE

Regie: Fritz Lang

BEHIND THE POSTERS: I love the style of vintage movie and propaganda posters from the early twentieth century. The artists were selective or minimal with their use of color—European artists in particular used very distinct color palettes and combinations of colors. Often times the subject matter was distorted and exaggerated for impact and custom illustrations and aggressive typography were dominant.

I was inspired by the intense/dark imagery on the original posters for *M* and *Le Corbeau* and wanted to create my own interpretation. Both movies were quite controversial for their time. In fact, it was documented that some of the directors and actors were persecuted for spotlighting such taboo subject matter.

Le Corbeau 11 x 14 in (28 x 36 cm)

UN FILM FRANÇAIS FAIT DEDANS MCMXLIII

RÉGALEZ-VOUS AVEC CE FILM POLITIQUEMENT INCORRECT

LE CORBEAU
HENRI-GEORGES COUZOT

DR RÉMY GERMAIN
PIERRE FRESNAY

DENISE SAILLENS
GINETTE LECLERC

MARIE CORBIN
HÉLÉNA MANSON

LE SOUS-PRÉFET
PIERRE BERTIN

ROLANDE SAILLENS
LILIANE MAIGNÉ

FRANÇOIS
ROGER BLIN

DESIGN FIRM Very Creative
LOCATION Cleveland Heights, Ohio / US
SITE Vervcreative.com

INFLUENCES: Shepard Fairey, Leonetto Cappiello, Quentin Tarantino.

PREFERRED MEDIUM: Digital layering/rendering in Photoshop. Photography.

a Woody Allen film

&

LOVE AND DEATH

WOODY ALLEN   DIANE KEATON

A JACK ROLLINS · CHARLES H. JOFFE PRODUCTION

BEHIND THE POSTER: *Love and Death* is one of Woody Allen's funniest films, but it didn't seem like the type of film that could be easily marketed since it's so cartoonish and hard to translate to a still image. I took that as a challenge: to come up with piece of artwork that could match the playful tone of the film.

INFLUENCES: I'm a fan of Saul Bass and Bauhaus. I think that poster design has become too loud and homogenous, and many of my favorite one-sheets are from the '70s or earlier.

FAVORITE FILM / GENRE: The Coen Brothers' films, particularly *Fargo*.

PREFERRED MEDIUM: A combination of traditional media and Photoshop, although I prefer to complete the majority of it outside of computer software.

ADDITIONAL REMARKS: I think that minimalist poster design is refreshing, but shouldn't be used as a crutch. A lot of minimalist poster design only stands out because we're used to loud, busy posters. It's not enough for a minimal poster to catch your attention in a sea of maximal posters. When you put it in a collection of similar posters, is it still effective?

Capote

Director: Bennett Miller

Writers: Dan Futterman (screenplay)
Gerald Clarke (book)

Stars:Philip Seymour Hoffman,
Clifton Collins Jr. and Catherine Keener

LOCATION Denver, Colorado / US

SITE Forestknauffdesigns.tumblr.com

BEHIND THE POSTER: I have always loved how weird Capote was, and that's why I chose to do a poster for the movie. I'm a huge fan of the film.
INFLUENCES: Wes Anderson has been a huge influence. I find myself watching his films far too often.

FAVORITE FILM / GENRE: My favorite film has to be *Moonrise Kingdom*. You can always tell a Wes Anderson film by its camera work.
FIRST FILM: The first film that I can remember seeing was *Grumpy Old Men*. It will always have a special place in my heart.
PREFERRED MEDIUM: I prefer to work in Adobe Illustrator.

Adam Pobiak

Repo Man
17 × 23 in (42 × 59 cm)

LOCATION London / UK (originally from Pittsburgh, Pennsylvania / US)

SITE Pobiak.com

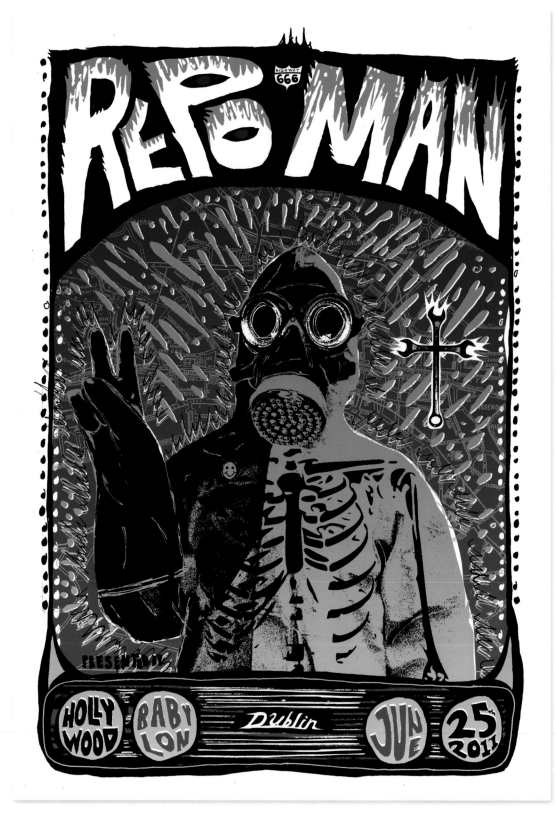

BEHIND THE POSTER: I was commissioned by Hollywood Babylon to create *Repo Man* for their screening on June 25, 2011. It's one of my all-time favorite films, and I developed about seven different designs here. There was so much in *Repo Man* to run with that it was hard to decide on the final piece.

INFLUENCES: Most of my influences come from poster art and music. I love all of the psychedelic '60s posters, and of course there are several great artists around today that I drool over. I also like faces. There is a face on nearly every print I've done in some form or another.

FAVORITE FILM / GENRE: I'm a sci-fi/fantasy guy at heart. It's mildly embarrassing, but I'm sure *The Neverending Story* is the film that I've seen the most in my lifetime. I won't tell you how many times that might be.

FIRST FILM: *Return of the Jedi* is the first film that I remember seeing in the cinema, but I suspect that there was a slew of less memorable kids' stuff before that.

PREFERRED MEDIUM: I always silkscreen all of my work by hand.

172

Derek Gabryszak

ALIAS	thatsthewayitgoes
LOCATION	New York / US
SITE	Thatsthewayitgoes.com

Continued from page 10

BEHIND THE POSTER: I designed *Maniac* for the Coolidge Corner Theater in Boston, Massachusetts. It was for one of their @fter Midnite screenings, and they had participation from Blue Underground [an entertainment company releasing cult classics on Blu-ray/DVD] while *Maniac* was on its 30th anniversary tour. I'm absolutely a fan of this film...now. The plot is a kind of weak (it was essentially a character study for Joe Spinell), but I love films like this—essentially a twisted version of character study. To be honest, I don't naturally gravitate towards horror films. I've definitely become a fan, though, and love designing posters for them.

LOCATION Saffron Walden / UK

SITE Excites.co.uk + Rareminimum.com

Vertigo
18 × 24 in (46 × 61 cm)

BEHIND THE POSTERS: Both films are great. I especially love the way that they grab hold and totally captivate you, whilst at the same time dragging you into the fear. *Vertigo* is one of my favorite films of all time, and my second favorite Hitchcock movie to *North by Northwest*. Time permitting, I could create posters all day long for them.

I opted for geometric designs in both of these, as I felt that this style fit both pictures rather well. I'm sure that at some point I will revisit *Vertigo* and put a different spin on it.

LOCATION Saffron Walden / UK

SITE Excites.co.uk + Rareminimum.com

Requiem for a Dream
18 × 24 in (46 × 61 cm)

A FILM BY DARREN ARONOFSKY

REQUIEM FOR A DREAM

ARTISAN ENTERTAINMENT AND THOUSAND WORDS PRESENTS A SIBLING/PROTOZOA PRODUCED IN ASSOCIATION WITH INDUSTRY AND BANDEIRA ENTERTAINMENT
A FILM BY DARREN ARONOFSKY "REQUIEM FOR A DREAM" ELLEN BURSTYN   JARED LETO   JENNIFER CONNELLY MARLOW WAYANS
EXECUTIVE PRODUCERS NICK WECHSLER   BEAU FLYNN   STEFAN SIMCHOWITZ CO-EXECUTIVE PRODUCERS BEN BARENHOLTZ CO-PRODUCERS RANDY SIMON   JOHAN SMITH
SCOTT VOGEL   SCOTT FRANKLIN LINE PRODUCER ANN RUARK ORIGINAL SCORE CLINT MANSELL WITH STRING QUARTETS PERFORMED BY KRONOS QUARTET COSTUME DESIGNER LAURA JEAN SHANNON
PRODUCTION DESIGNER JAMES CHINLUND EDITED BY JAY RABINOWITZ, A.C.E. DIRECTOR OF PHOTOGRAPHY MATTHEW LIBATIQUE PRODUCED BY ERIC WATSON AND PALMER WEST
BASED UPON THE BOOK BY HERBERT SELBY JR. SCREENPLAY BY HURBERT SELBY JR. AND DARREN ARONOFSKY DIRECTED BY DARREN ARONOFSKY

INFLUENCES: I am most influenced by designers and directors who are very minimal and don't come across as trying too hard—designers like Saul Bass, whose designs took a lot of time to perfect but look simple and effortless.

PREFERRED MEDIUM: Digital. I can draw, and I love the feel of paper, but I love the undo function far too much.

DESIGN FIRM &co Design

LOCATION Atlanta, Georgia / US

SITE Andcodesign.com

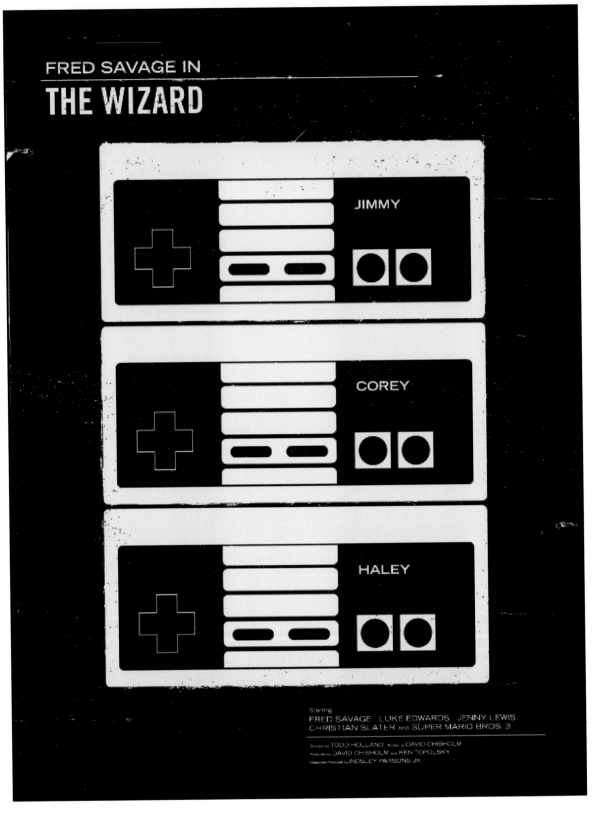

FRED SAVAGE IN

THE WIZARD

JIMMY

COREY

HALEY

Starring
FRED SAVAGE LUKE EDWARDS JENNY LEWIS
CHRISTIAN SLATER and SUPER MARIO BROS. 3

Directed by TODD HOLLAND Written by DAVID CHISHOLM
Produced by DAVID CHISHOLM and KEN TOPOLSKY
Executive Producer LINDSLEY PARSONS JR.

BEHIND THE POSTERS: I started the Rectangular Film project as a way to fill time during lulls in client work. I enjoyed the challenge of trying to not only capture a film in one image, but to also have that image conform to a rectangle right in the middle of the poster. From there I started listing some of my favorite movies, and whether or not I could fit them into the Rectangular Film concept. The NES [Nintendo Entertainment System] controllers seemed like a perfect fit for *The Wizard*. And *JFK* [right] was chosen because it is one of my wife's favorite movies.

INFLUENCES: Influences are everywhere. I'm constantly looking at other designers' work. But most of the time I just try to make something that will impress my friends.

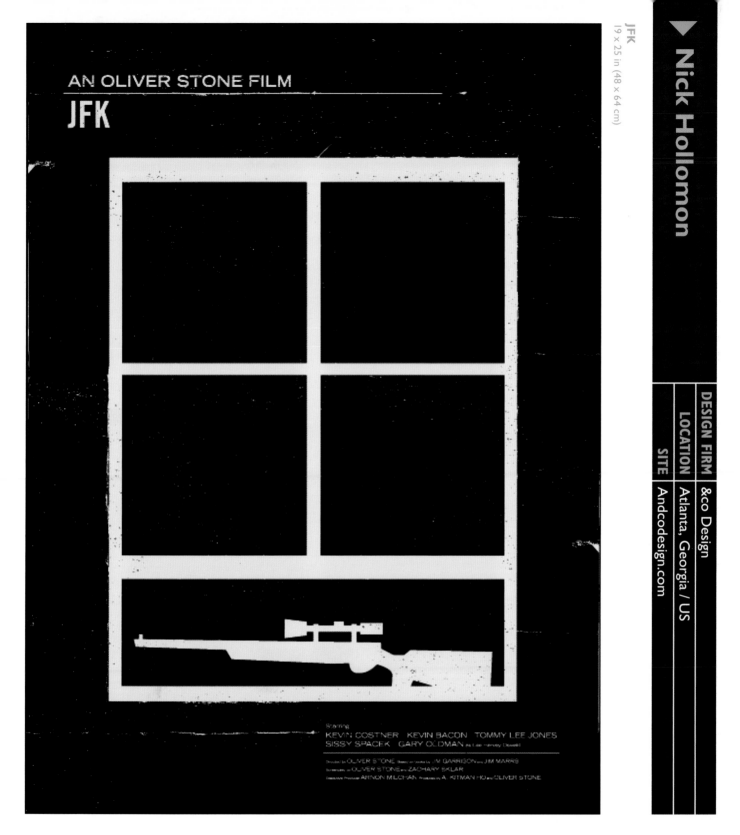

AN OLIVER STONE FILM

JFK

Starring
KEVIN COSTNER   KEVIN BACON   TOMMY LEE JONES
SISSY SPACEK   GARY OLDMAN as Lee Harvey Oswald

Directed by OLIVER STONE Based on books by JIM GARRISON and JIM MARRS
Screenplay by OLIVER STONE and ZACHARY SKLAR
Executive Producer ARNON MILCHAN Produced by A. KITMAN HO and OLIVER STONE

DESIGN FIRM	&co Design
LOCATION	Atlanta, Georgia / US
SITE	Andcodesign.com

FAVORITE FILM / GENRE: *Star Wars: Episode V – The Empire Strikes Back* or *Predator.* Both are absolute masterpieces for entirely different reasons.
FIRST FILM: The 1933 version of *King Kong*, at my grandfather's house.

PREFERRED MEDIUM: Screen printing.
ADDITIONAL REMARKS: I have the best wife and the two coolest kids in the entire world.

DESIGN FIRM Wonderbros

LOCATION Houston, Texas / US

SITE Wonderbros.com

BEHIND THE POSTERS: I'm a huge fan of both of these films. *The Lost Boys* [right] tells one of the greatest modern day vampire stories. It has big moussed-out hair, blood, gore, exploding vampires, and comic books. *The Road Warrior* is just one bad ass flick.

INFLUENCES: I'm heavily influenced by the works of Saul Bass, Andy Warhol, Alex Ross, and my brother, Mike Esparza. I love watching films by Alfred Hitchcock, John Carpenter, and Kevin Smith. I also read and collect comic books.

FAVORITE FILM / GENRE: My all-time favorite film is *Escape from New York*. It's the one poster that I've yet to finish. I have a ton of ideas and sketches for it. I just want it to be perfect. Favorite movie genre: thrillers.

FIRST FILM: John Carpenter's *The Thing*. My father took my brother and I, and it scared the crap out of me. I loved it!

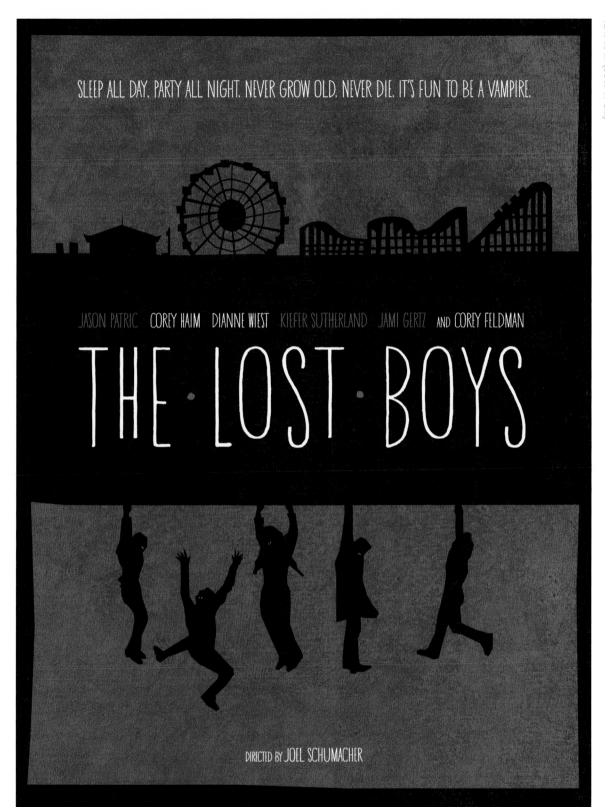

Matthew Esparza

The Lost Boys
12 × 16 in (30 × 41 cm)

DESIGN FIRM Wonderbros
LOCATION Houston, Texas / US
SITE Wonderbros.com

PREFERRED MEDIUM: I love to sketch. Ideas are always brewing, so I carry a pen and a small notepad with me everywhere I go. When I'm working on an idea for a poster, I usually start with a sketch. Then I recreate that concept on the computer. I build everything in vector first (Illustrator), then usually apply some final touches, effects, and textures in Photoshop.

ADDITIONAL REMARKS: When I'm developing a poster, I try to think of a story that I'd like to tell visually. Something that will make perfect sense to anyone who has seen the film, or that will create interest for someone who hasn't.

Harry and the Hendersons
11 x 17 in (28 x 43 cm)

BEHIND THE POSTER: My sister, my brother, and I loved *Harry and the Hendersons* as children. My sister especially loved it and would watch a *Harry* VHS tape on nearly a daily basis. So now every scene is forever imprinted in my brain. I made this print for her as a birthday gift.

INFLUENCES: I wanted the poster to have the feel of a classic Universal Monster movie poster from the '30s. I thought it would be fun to imagine the movie as a scary horror film rather than a family friendly comedy. For the human characters I was going for a less exaggerated version of an Al Hirschfeld caricature. The typography is definitely influenced by the classic, cut paper look of a Saul Bass design.

FIRST FILM: *Unico in the Island of Magic*. I remember being fascinated by it but also very scared by the evil wizards.

PREFERRED MEDIUM: Brush pen and Adobe Illustrator.

ADDITIONAL REMARKS: As a strange twist, I now live a few blocks away from where the Henderson's home scenes were filmed, in the Wallingford neighborhood of Seattle. Their home and the nosy neighbor's house are still there.

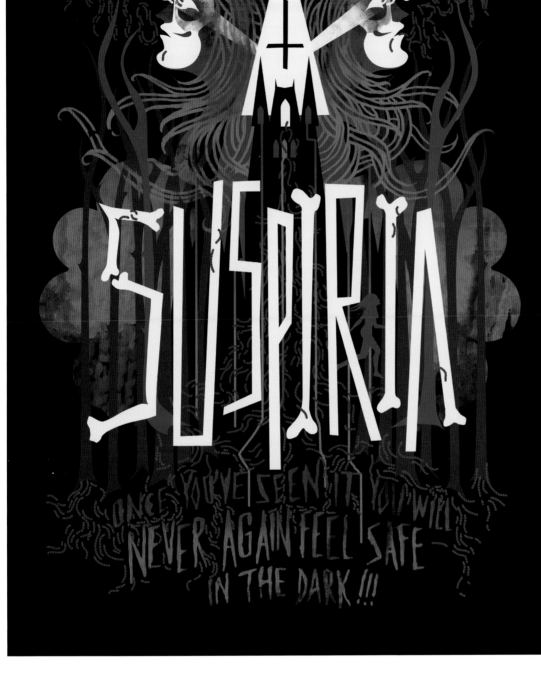

DESIGNERS	Sonny Day and Biddy Maroney
LOCATION	Newtown, Sydney / Australia
SITE	Wbyk.com.au

BEHIND THE POSTER: We were approached by Darren Firth to create a piece for his Now Showing exhibition in London in 2008. He asked everyone in the show to do their take on a cult movie poster. We decided on *Suspiria,* based solely on Sonny constantly playing the soundtrack. Sonny had loved the film for years, but I hadn't seen it. We watched it together, and since then, *Suspiria* (and all of the subsequent Dario Argento films that Sonny has shown me) have influenced a great deal of our work.

FAVORITE FILM / GENRE: [Sonny]: I would never be able to pick a favorite, but I am constantly watching horror movies. [Biddy]: *Amadeus, Jaws, Gosford Park, Rebecca*…and my favorite genre is murder mysteries.
FIRST FILM: [Sonny]: It was either *Star Wars* or *Laser Blast.* [Biddy]: My earliest film memory is Shelley Duvall and a giant squid in *Popeye.*
PREFERRED MEDIUM: Sonny works in pencils, paint, markers, and screen prints. Biddy works on a computer or with ink and a brush.

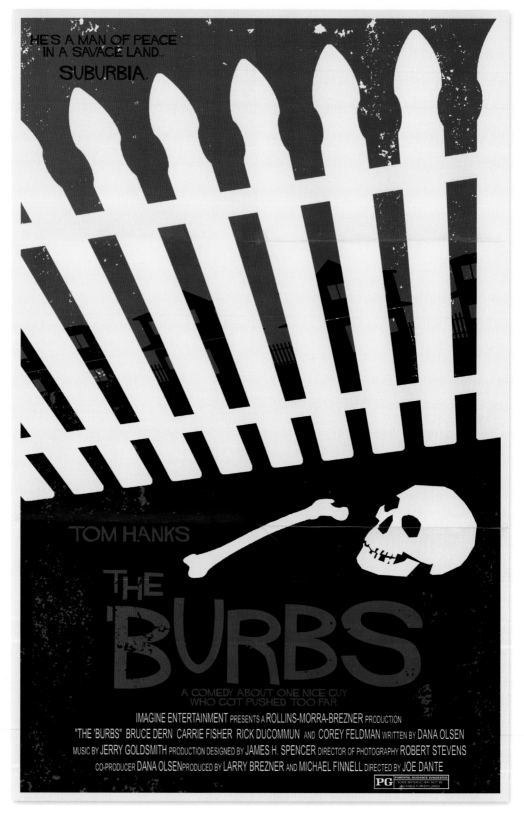

Continued from page 49

The Help
13 x 19 in (33 x 48 cm)

The Help

STARRING JESSICA CHASTAIN VIOLA DAVIS BRYCE DALLAS HOWARD ALLISON JANNEY OCTAVIA SPENCER EMMA STONE
PRODUCED BY BRUNSON GREEN CHRIS COLUMBUS MICHAEL BARNATHAN
WRITTEN AND DIRECTED BY TATE TAYLOR

LOCATION Detroit, Michigan / US

SITE Hunterlangston.com

BEHIND THE POSTERS: Every year I create a series of posters for the Oscars and their best picture nominees. It's a personal challenge to see all of the films and to come up with designs in the month between their nomination and the show. I really enjoyed both films here, but *The Artist* [right] was my favorite. It was a beautiful and timeless film that showed how much emotion can be conveyed without dialogue.

INFLUENCES: I'm influenced by artists like Olly Moss, Jason Munn, Shigeo Fukuda, and Saul Bass. Film directors: Quentin Tarantino, David Fincher, John Hughes, and Cameron Crowe.

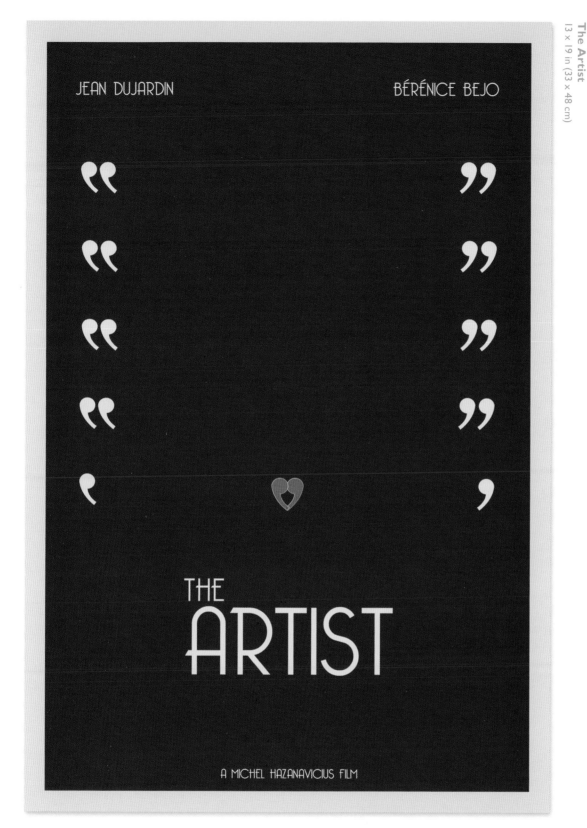

Hunter Langston

LOCATION Detroit, Michigan / US

SITE Hunterlangston.com

FAVORITE FILM / GENRE: I like any film that's visually stimulating and effectively tells a story.
FIRST FILM: *E.T.*
PREFERRED MEDIUM: Print.

ADDITIONAL REMARKS: Alternative and minimalist movie posters have grown in popularity because designers have taken them back to being an artistic and creative medium, rather than just a marketing and promotional tool.

Kako and Carlos Bêla

Blade Runner
23 × 33 in (58 × 84 cm)

LOCATION São Paulo, São Paulo / Brazil

SITE Kakofonia.com + Carlosbela.com

MAN HAS MADE HIS MATCH
... NOW IT'S HIS PROBLEM

HARRISON FORD IS

BLADE RUNNER

screenplay by HAMPTON FANCHER &
DAVID PEOPLES
executive producers BRIAN KELLY &
HAMPTON FANCHER
visual effects by DOUGLAS TRUMBULL
original music composed by VANGELIS
associate producer IVOR POWELL
produced by MICHAEL DEELEY
directed by RIDLEY SCOTT

BEHIND THE POSTERS: [Carlos]: Kako and I have known each other for a long time. Before we worked together on *Blade Runner,* we used to meet for a late night cup of coffee here in São Paulo. We always wanted to work on a project together, but never had the opportunity. [Kako]: Carlos and I were looking for an excuse to work together and I was glad that the opportunity came up for such a great project. We have different styles in our everyday work, but we both share the same vision regarding graphic design.

When I showed Carlos the owl idea, he came up with a few designs, and the very last one was a beautiful title design, and suddenly it all fit. This poster mixes our "style DNA" together perfectly. Later we revisited the poster and came up with two new variations: *The Director's Cut* [right], which has the original combination of orange and dark color that Carlos suggested in his first drafts, and *The Final Cut,* with a yellow and black combo that I wanted to try.

LOCATION	São Paulo, São Paulo / Brazil
SITE	Kakofonia.com + Carlosbela.com

INFLUENCES: [Kako]: The list is long, but every now and then I obsess over some artists. This week I'm all over Ashley Wood's work, but next week…who knows? [Carlos]: Everything, everywhere.

FAVORITE FILM / GENRE: [Kako]: *Blade Runner* is at the top of my list, and I think Ridley Scott's early films are all great. Also, Wes Anderson is a film director that I like very much nowadays; all of his movies are perfect. [Carlos]: It's impossible for me to choose a single film, but I can try: *Murder by Death, The Shining, Vertigo, Manhattan, The Pillow Book, Lost Highway*…just to name a few.

FIRST FILM: [Kako]: *Pete's Dragon*, I think. [Carlos]: *Singing in the Rain*. My father loved the MGM musicals.

PREFERRED MEDIUM: [Kako]: Digital illustration. [Carlos]: My main medium is video. Broadcast design, animation, design in motion, movie and TV titles, etc.

ALIAS	akaStarWarskid
LOCATION	Austin, Texas / US
SITE	Akastarwarskid.tumblr.com + Hipster-movie-posters.tumblr.com

Continued from page 163

BEHIND THE POSTERS: *Drive* and *Dial M* [right] are part of a project I started called Hipster Movie Posters. With the affluence of hipster design out there and my love for cinema, I thought it would be cool to start designing posters as though each of these films was an indie movie that only hipsters were attending. Being a filmmaker as well, each of these films have influenced me one way or another.

Dial M for Murder
11 x 17 in (28 x 43 cm)

ALIAS	akaStarWarskid
LOCATION	Austin, Texas / US
SITE	Akastarwarskid.tumblr.com + Hipster-movie-posters.tumblr.com

Edward Scissorhands
11 × 17 in (28 × 43 cm)

ALIAS	Cynic with a Pencil
LOCATION	New York, New York / US
SITE	Cynicwithapencil.blogspot.com + Cynicwithapencil.tumblr.com

SHE NEVER SAW HIM AGAIN.
NOT AFTER THAT NIGHT.

"FAREWELL EDWARD"   20/30

Continued from page 81

BEHIND THE POSTERS: The *Edward Scissorhands* piece was for an *Edward Scissorhands* 20th anniversary show at Gallery Nucleus. I was invited by artist Seb Mesnard to participate, along with a group of other talented illustrators whom he had chosen.

Army of Darkness [right] was an event poster for a monthly film at the Trocadero Theatre in Philadelphia. The event was called Midnight Movies @ The Troc. They asked me to contribute the *Army of Darkness* poster after seeing my *Kill Bill* one-sheet a month prior.

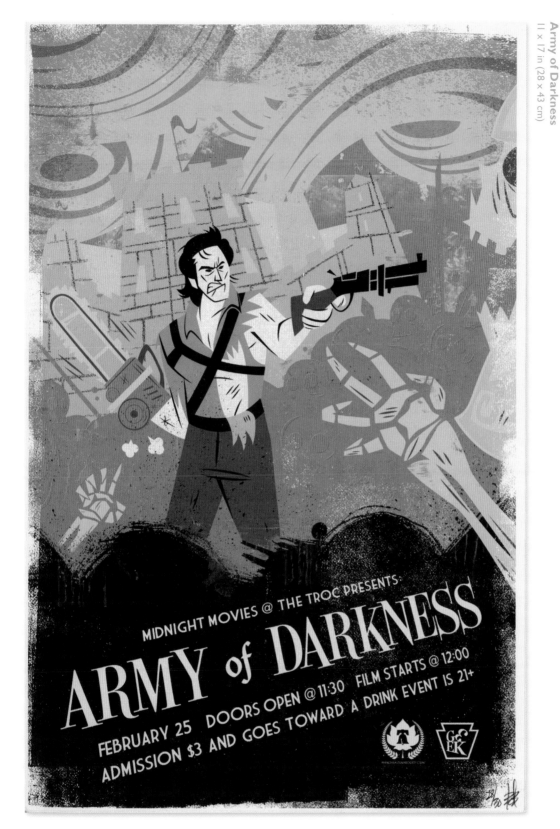

► Bobby O'Herlihy

ALIAS | Cynic with a Pencil
LOCATION | New York, New York / US
SITE | Cynicwithapencil.blogspot.com
+ Cynicwithapencil.tumblr.com

Christopher Monro DeLorenzo

O Brother, Where Art Thou?
Unprinted / animated GIF

LOCATION Boston, Massachusetts / US

SITE Chrisdelorenzo.com

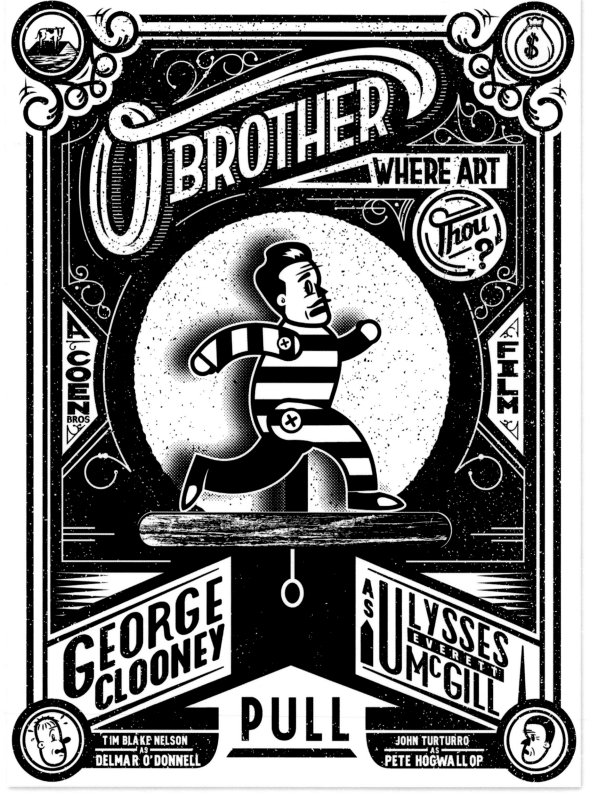

BEHIND THE POSTER: The poster was part of a larger project called The Silver Screen Society, where a new film is picked every month and illustrators and designers are asked to create an art piece based around that film.

INFLUENCES: Herbert Leupin, Donald Brun, Saul Steinberg, John Wesley, William Morris, Seymour Chwast, Jerry Garcia.

FAVORITE FILM / GENRE: Drama/suspense or anything by Christopher Nolan. I love films that are heavy in style, like *Revolver*, *Running Scared*, *Cosmopolis*, and *Drive*.

FIRST FILM: *Rad.*

PREFERRED MEDIUM: Pen and paper. Adobe Illustrator.

BEHIND THE POSTER: I'm a huge fan of The Coen Brothers films and also Jeff Bridges, so when I heard they were reuniting for a remake of *True Grit,* I was inspired to design a poster reflecting its character. I love the rugged art direction and attitude of the film, so I tried to sum this up visually in the form of Rooster Cogburn's real weapon of choice.

INFLUENCES: Herb Lubalin, Lucian Freud, Noma Bar.
FAVORITE FILM / GENRE: *Blade Runner.*
FIRST FILM: I remember watching John Carpenter's *The Thing* with my Dad when I was *way* too young.
PREFERRED MEDIUM: Digital media.

Inglourious Basterds
12 x 18 in (30 x 46 cm)

LOCATION Washington, DC / USA

SITE Chasematt.com

INGLOURIOUS
BASTERDS

BEHIND THE POSTERS: Both of these films are simply good movies on a lot of different levels. I've always kept a long running list of potential titles (to create posters for) in the margins of my sketchbooks, and these were two of the first ones I wrote down that I didn't later go back and scratch out. Ironically, I didn't much enjoy *8 1/2* [right] when I first saw it; we screened it in a first-year university film class and I—along with the rest of my classmates— nearly fell asleep. Several years later, I discovered that throughout the entire shooting of the movie, Fellini attached a note to the camera that read "Remember, this is a comedy." After that, it just sort of clicked for me.

INFLUENCES: People and relationships are probably the most bottomless source of inspiration, truth, humility, and joy. If I had nothing else to observe for the rest of my life, I could probably be happy just watching people go about their lives. There's a subtlety in the mundane that's truly poetic.

As far as creative folks go, it's mostly a mix of writers, designers, and filmmakers, not limited to but certainly comprising F. Scott Fitzgerald, David Fincher, Woody Allen, Saul Bass, and Pablo Picasso.

That being said, I try as hard as I can not to draw influence from other artwork. As any other creative-minded person will attest, it's an easier-said-than-done sort of mantra (that's a lie; it's completely impossible), but your best work will always come when you finally divorce yourself from the "I want to make something that looks like this other thing" mindset.

FAVORITE FILM / GENRE: Anything that's emotive. Thankfully, that's an ambiguous word and can mean just about anything. *Annie Hall* is probably my single favorite.

FIRST FILM: The first movie that I remember slipping into the VHS player is *Star Wars*. My parents had taped our copy off of television and to this day, I still anticipate all the commercial breaks when I watch it.

PREFERRED MEDIUM: I work mostly on the computer but would be panicked without a sketchbook.

Halloween
18 x 24 in (46 x 61 cm)

Ryan Black

LOCATION Chicago, Illinois / US

SITE Ryanblackdesigns.com

BEHIND THE POSTERS: Being a self-proclaimed horror movie geek, *Halloween* is one of my all-time favorite movies, not to mention a staple of the genre. I also love all three of the *Evil Dead* [right] movies, and have a soft spot for survivor horror.

INFLUENCES: Visually, I love every second of a Ridley Scott or Stanley Kubrick film. More recently, filmmakers like Paul Thomas Anderson, Darren Aronofsky, Kim Ji-woon, Rian Johnson, Park Chan-wook, and Nicholas Winding Refn have all been producing stunning movies.

As far as movie posters go, as cliché of an answer as it is, the work that Saul Bass did is still about as good as it gets for me. Add to that his opening credits work, especially on *Psycho* and *North by Northwest,* and he is pretty much untouchable.

FAVORITE FILM / GENRE: I can remember going to the video store as a kid every weekend and wandering through the horror section, checking out every VHS case. Luckily, I had parents who were OK with allowing their 8-year-old to rent what most people considered offensive trash. They also had the common sense to sit me down at an early age and talk to me about what was real and what wasn't, rather than just blindly shielding me from everything.

196

My favorite film would have to be *Psycho* (with *Alien* nipping close at its heels). The story, the direction, the acting—all perfection. I don't think that a movie will ever come close to that caliber again.

FIRST FILM: That would be *Alien*. Actually, watching *Alien* is my first fully formed memory, period. I have watched it more times than I can count. A gothic, haunted house movie in space? Pure genius.

PREFERRED MEDIUM: All of my posters are created using Adobe Illustrator and Photoshop.

ADDITIONAL REMARKS: I am thrilled that this book was published. Another step forward in the alternative/independent movie poster movement.

Behind the Mask
27 x 40 in (69 x 102 cm)

DESIGN FIRM	Slasher Design
LOCATION	Lawrence, Kansas / US
SITE	Osbourndraw.com + Slasherdesign.blogspot.com

Continued from page 126

BEHIND THE POSTERS: For *Behind the Mask*, I was contacted by the director, Scott Glosserman, about designing a poster design for the theatrical re-release of the movie. So, it was created both to promote the original film and was sold as a limited edition poster to help raise funds for a sequel.

Hatchet [right], as with *Silent Night, Deadly Night* [see page 126] was created for Fright Rags.

Hatchet
18 x 24 in (46 x 61 cm)

WARNING!
CONTAINS EXTREME VISIONS OF
VIOLENCE NUDITY AND GORE

STAY OUT
OF THE
SWAMP!

OSBOURN

HATCHET

JOEL DAVID MOORE • TAMARA FELDMAN • DEON RICHMOND • MERCEDES MCNAB • PARRY SHEN • JOLEIGH FIOREVANTI • JOEL MURRAY
RICHARD RIEHLE • PATRIKA DARBO • JOSHUA LEONARD • TONY TODD WITH ROBERT ENGLUND AND KANE HODDER AS VICTOR CROWLEY
CASTING BY SHANNON MAKHANIAN COSTUMES DESIGNED BY HEATHER SLADINSKI COMPOSER ANDY GARFIELD FILM EDITOR CHRISTOPHER ROTH
SPECIAL MAKE-UP EFFECTS BY JOHN CARL BUECHLER AND MAGICAL MEDIA INDUSTRIES PRODUCTION DESIGNER BRYAN MCBRIEN
DIRECTOR OF PHOTOGRAPHY WILL BARRATT EXECUTIVE PRODUCERS ANDREW MYSKO ROMAN KINDRACHUK PRODUCERS SARAH ELBERT SCOTT ALTOMARE
PRODUCED BY COREY NEAL WRITTEN AND DIRECTED BY ADAM GREEN

arieScope PICTURES   FRIGHT RAGS   SLASHER   R RESTRICTED   UNDER 17 REQUIRES ACCOMPANYING
PARENT OR ADULT GUARDIAN

DESIGN FIRM	Slasher Design
LOCATION	Lawrence, Kansas / US
SITE	Osbourndraw.com + Slasherdesign.blogspot.com

Prometheus
18 × 24 in (46 × 61 cm)

LOCATION Los Angeles, California / US

SITE Midmarauder.tumblr.com

BEHIND THE POSTERS: I have been a loyal Ridley Scott fan since I was a kid, and *Blade Runner* is (and always has been) my favorite film of all time. Ridley Scott is a true visionary force of nature.

INFLUENCES: Rob Jones, Neil Kellerhouse, Print Mafia, Paul Thomas Anderson, Peckinpah, Soderbergh, Kubrick, and Robert Altman.

FAVORITE FILM / GENRE: Film noir and westerns.
FIRST FILM: *A Clockwork Orange*, at the tender age of 3.
PREFERRED MEDIUM: Digital, screen print, cut, and paste.

ADDITIONAL REMARKS: I was completely surprised by the reaction that I received from my *Prometheus* series, and made plenty of friends as a result of it. I was told by a good source that worked on the film that Ridley himself saw them. That is the greatest reward!

DESIGN FIRM Visuals By Linda
LOCATION The Netherlands
SITE Visualsbylinda.com

BEHIND THE POSTER: Marie Antoinette's character in the film is fascinating. She was famous and rich for basically doing nothing; a one-dimensional person with a limited range of interests and skills. In today's world we have a gigantic influx of similar individuals in pop culture. With very limited artistic resources, some reach stardom because they are backed by marketing machines with deep pockets. From that perspective, this film bridges the seemingly large gap between the past and present.

With this poster I attempted to visualize that bridge as well. I wanted to design a classical, feminine face, but in a fresh way by using metaphors in the wig's design and the overall color palette.

INFLUENCES: I prefer visuals over words, and less is more. Stanley Kubrick is a great example. He provides the most complete cinematic experience, from the visuals to the underlying thematic statements, but it's all very subtle and layered.

FAVORITE FILM / GENRE: *2001: A Space Odyssey* is one of my favorites. Again, the perfect combination between minimalism and great visuals. But I also loved *Drive*, where a violent film was also able to be so touching. Movies like these transcend genres and define new ones.

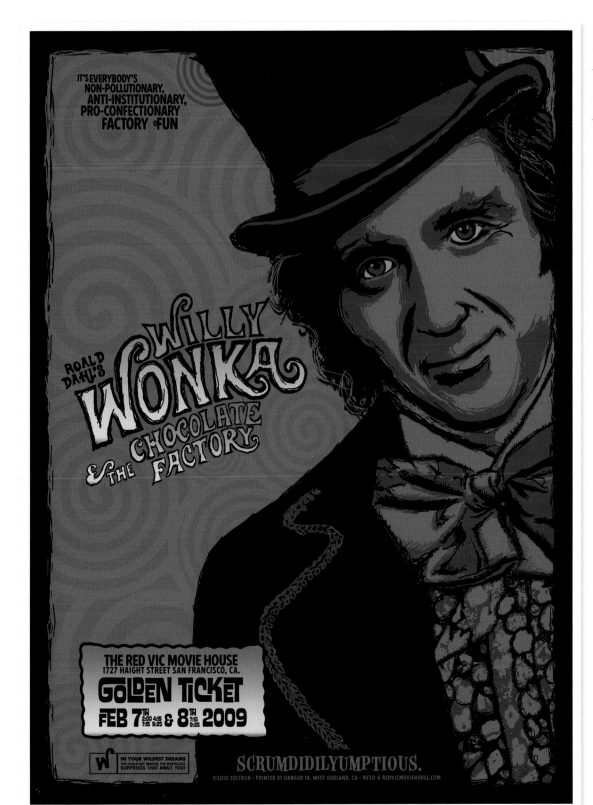

LOCATION	San Francisco Bay Area, California / US
SITE	Zoltron.com + Stickerobot.com

BEHIND THE POSTER: To celebrate their 30-year anniversary, The Red Vic commissioned my friends Ron Donovan and Dave Hunter to curate a series of limited edition, hand-pulled silkscreen posters for movies shown throughout the year. They sold the posters after each showing and generated a little cash to help keep the doors open. *Willy Wonka* is an all-time classic. I tried to show Wonka's twisted, darker side in a subtle way—that unpredictable nature that Gene Wilder portrayed so well. You never knew if he was going to hug you or have his blue henchlings hold your head under fudge sauce until you stopped kicking.

FAVORITE FILM / GENRE: Tough question. I don't know what my favorite color is either. I'd say more Jim Jarmusch, less James Cameron. More Tom Waits, less Tom Cruise.

FIRST FILM: My mom's water broke during *The Last Picture Show*. I guess that was my first movie. My dad used to bring me to any film he was seeing, regardless of how old I was. I remember seeing *Apocalypse Now* when I was seven. My parents believed in exposing their kids to everything. Now that I think about it, that explains why I break out in hives when I see camouflage.

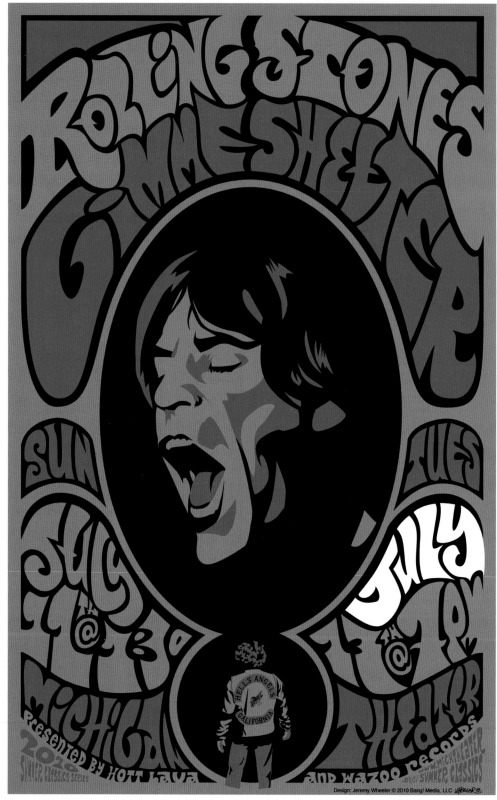

Gimme Shelter
11 x 17 in (28 x 43 cm)

Jeremy Wheeler

DESIGN FIRM Bang! Media
LOCATION Ann Arbor, Michigan / US
SITE Thisisbangmedia.com

BEHIND THE POSTERS: *Gimme Shelter* was done in conjunction with The Michigan Theater and the experimental film happening, *Hott Lava*. I approached it as if it were a 1960s Grande Ballroom rock poster—especially since Ann Arbor and Detroit were the mecca of revolutionary rock 'n' roll back then.

The *Velvet Goldmine* prints [right] were part of a fun project where fictional movie bands are given gig poster treatment. The Brian Slade piece riffs on a classic Bowie logo, while Curt Wild is a direct homage to an Iggy Pop poster by the great Gary Grimshaw, a renowned Detroit artist whose incredible body of work acts a constant source of inspiration.

INFLUENCES: Other than Grimshaw, Mark Arminski is another Detroit artist who's right up there in my top ten. Billy Perkins, Brian Ewing, Adam Pobiak, and Shawn Knight are all nailing it in the gig poster world. As for movie artists, Jay Shaw, Phantom City Collective, Brandon Schaefer, and Olly Moss slay me, though I'd be silly not to mention Graham Humphries, Drew Struzan, Bob Peak, and Saul Bass as artists whose one-sheets work are ingrained in my movie-loving DNA.

Velvet Goldmine 9 × 24 in (23 × 61 cm)

Velvet Goldmine 9 × 24 in (23 × 61 cm)

▼ Jeremy Wheeler

DESIGN FIRM Bang! Media

LOCATION Ann Arbor, Michigan / US

SITE Thisisbangmedia.com

FAVORITE FILM / GENRE: I fiercely love horror films, but if I'm not down with the aesthetics, I just can't hang. Popcorn movies, when done right, can still get me pumped, as do most flicks where things explode in non-shaky ways. Favorite films are *Jaws* and *Carlito's Way.* I really do believe that I have one great *Carlito's Way* poster in me...or dozens. Many would feature Sean Penn's hair.

FIRST FILM: *Jaws.* My family made sure that I knew that Quint was spitting up ketchup at the end. I later went to college focusing on makeup FX before I remembered how more much I liked drawing monsters rather than making them out of latex (though getting taught by a Romero alum in Pittsburgh was a definite highlight).

ADDITIONAL REMARKS: This is really an amazing time to be a poster artist. I'd love a future where more artistic work graces poster frames in theater chains, but for the time being, it's great to hear from individual fans that are geeked to showcase your work on their walls—one of the highest forms of flattery. I wish I had more walls to decorate myself!

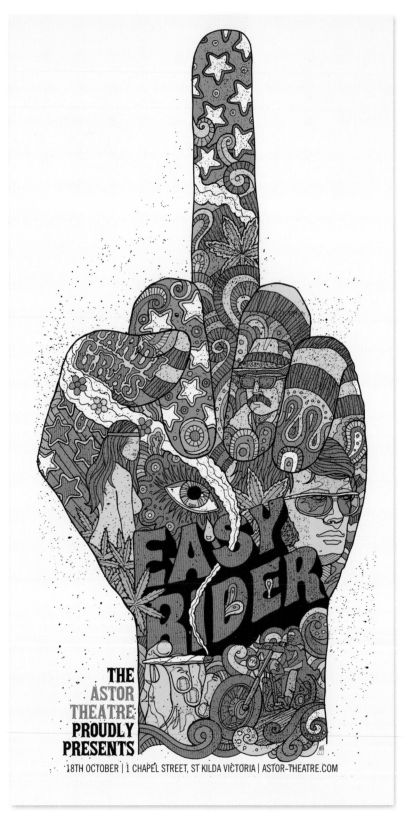

Easy Rider
16 × 36 in (41 × 91 cm)

DESIGNERS Robert Lee and Mark McDevitt
LOCATION Atlanta, Georgia / US
SITE Methanestudios.com

BEHIND THE POSTER: The Astor Theatre [Victoria, Australia] asked us to design this poster for film screenings.

INFLUENCES: [Robert]: The *Easy Rider* poster was designed to represent the time period and aesthetic of the 1960s. The movie is irreverent, so I used the ultimate iconic image of the middle finger to express that. Sex, drugs, and rock and roll! What more could I ask for in an assignment?

FAVORITE FILM / GENRE: [Robert]: I'm a huge horror and sci-fi fan, and definitely am inspired by classic horror: *Psycho, Halloween, Planet of the Apes, Alien, Jaws, The Outlaw Josey Wales*, etc.

FIRST FILM: [Robert]: *Jaws*, or perhaps the original *King Kong* (my brother had the poster on his wall back in the mid-'70s).

PREFERRED MEDIUM: [Robert]: Traditionally, medium would be acrylic and watercolor. Printing would be screen printing and letterpress.

ADDITIONAL REMARKS: [Robert]: Movie posters were a huge influence on me as a kid. Back then they were frequently illustrated, which mesmerized me…big-ass posters of fantastical imagery. It had always been a dream to design my own poster versions for some of my favorite films.

Harold and Maude
24 x 36 in (61 x 91 cm)

Harold
and
Maude

Bud Cort   Ruth Gordon

▼ **Ellen Surrey**

LOCATION Los Angeles, California / US

SITE EllenSurrey.com

BEHIND THE POSTER: I love *Harold and Maude*. The message is so pure and true, with two seemingly opposites falling in love. While the film ends on a bittersweet note, I always manage to walk away feeling a spark inside. So, with my poster I wanted to capture the spirit of the film in that true bittersweet fashion.

FIRST FILM: I remember watching *The Sound of Music* endlessly as a kid. I loved, and still love, Julie Andrews. At the time I wanted nothing more than to be the eighth von Trapp child.

PREFERRED MEDIUM: At the moment my favorite medium is gouache. I love the history it has in illustration and I just don't think you can beat some of the colors compared to other mediums.

ADDITIONAL REMARKS: When I discovered that Al Hirschfeld got his start in the movie poster business, I thought that it must be a dream job. To be able to combine two of my biggest loves, art and film, into a career would be amazing. When I created this poster for *Harold and Maude* I think a small part of me felt like I had achieved that dream. I hope that in the future I will have the opportunity to design additional posters.

207

Other Schiffer Books by the Author:
Put the Needle on the Record: The 1980s at 45 Revolutions Per Minute, 978-0-7643-3831-1, $39.99

Other Schiffer Books on Related Subjects:
Graphic Horror: Movie Monster Memories,
    978-0-7643-4082-6, $39.99
The World's Rarest Movie Posters, 978-0-7643-3498-6, $39.99
Hollywood Movie Posters: 1914–1990, 978-0-7643-2010-1, $49.95

Copyright © 2013 by Matthew Chojnacki

Library of Congress Control Number: 2013944509

Cover design by Steve Dressler (StevenDressler.com), based on the film *Taxi Driver*.

On the Back Cover:
Top row (left to right): *Blade Runner* / Kako & Carlos Bêla, *Repo Man* / Adam Pobiak, and *Revenge of the Cheerleaders* / Laurie Shipley.
Bottom row (left to right): *Rushmore* / Travis Price, *The Big Lebowski* / Ghoulish Gary Pullin, and *Die Hard* / Derek Chatwood.

Designed by Justin Watkinson
Type set in Gill Sans Std/Minion Pro

ISBN: 978-0-7643-4566-1
Printed in China

Published by Schiffer Publishing, Ltd.
4880 Lower Valley Road
Atglen, PA 19310
Phone: (610) 593-1777; Fax: (610) 593-2002
E-mail: Info@schifferbooks.com

For our complete selection of fine books on this and related subjects, please visit our website at www.schifferbooks.com. You may also write for a free catalog.

This book may be purchased from the publisher. Please try your bookstore first.

We are always looking for people to write books on new and related subjects. If you have an idea for a book, please contact us at proposals@schifferbooks.com.

Schiffer Publishing's titles are available at special discounts for bulk purchases for sales promotions or premiums. Special editions, including personalized covers, corporate imprints, and excerpts can be created in large quantities for special needs. For more information, contact the publisher.